Selected Poems
by
Fernando Pessoa

Selected Poems
by
Fernando Pessoa

including poems by his heteronyms

Alberto Caeiro

Ricardo Reis

Alvaro de Campos

*as well as some of his English
sonnets and selections from his letters*

translated by

Edwin Honig

with an Introduction by

Octavio Paz

THE SWALLOW PRESS INC.

CHICAGO

Published by
The Swallow Press Incorporated
1139 South Wabash Avenue
Chicago, Illinois 60605

This book is printed on 100% recycled paper.

Fernando Pessoa's poetry has been reprinted and translated by permission
of Louis Rosa for the Estate of Fernando Pessoa.

ISBN 0-8040-0520-6
LIBRARY OF CONGRESS CATALOG CARD NUMBER 75-150758

CONTENTS

Preface: Translator's Note ix

Introduction: Pessoa or the Imminence of the Unknown,
        by Octavio Paz 1

1. Alberto Caeiro

from *The Shepherd*

II. My glance is as clear as a sunflower 25
IX. I'm a shepherd 27
X. "Hello, shepherd, 27
XIV. Rhymes mean nothing to me 29
XXVIII. Today I read nearly two pages 29
XXX. If they want me to be a mystic, fine 31
XXXII. Yesterday afternoon a city man 31
XLIII. Rather the bird flying by 33
XLVIII. On a terribly clear day 35

from *Disjunctive Poems*

You tell me: but you're something more 37
The frightening reality of things 39

2. Ricardo Reis

from *Odes*

I the roses love in the gardens of Adonis 45
Now hoary gray descends upon the brows 45
Whatever stops is death, and is our death 45
Recalling who I was, I see somebody else 47
Lydia, when our Autumn comes 47
No one, in the vast and virgin jungle 47
Lydia, we know nothing. We are strangers 49
To be great, be whole 49
I ask the gods only to forget me 49
I only ask the gods to grant me 51

3. Alvaro de Campos

from *Poems*

I have a terrible cold   55
The sleep that comes over me   55
Salutation to Walt Whitman   57
Note   71
Psychotype   73
Poem in a Straight Line   75
Tobacco Shop   77
Maritime Ode   89

4. Fernando Pessoa

from *Uncollected Poems* (*1930-1935*)

Lightly, quickly, soft   147
She is singing, poor reaper   147
Cat, you tumble down the street   149
I'm so full of feeling   151
I sleep. If I dream, I do not know on waking   151
Autopsychography   153
This   153
We Took the Town after a Heavy Bombing   155
I'm a runaway   155

English Poems, from *35 Sonnets* (1918)

Sonnet IV: I could not think of thee as pieced rot   158
Sonnet VI: As a bad orator, badly o'er-book-skilled   158
Sonnet XII: As the lone, frighted user of a night-road   159
Sonnet XIV: We are born at sunset and we die ere noon   159
Sonnet XV: Like a bad suitor desperate and trembling   160
Sonnet XVII: My love, and not I, is the egoist   160
Sonnet XX: When in the widening circle of rebirth   161
Sonnet XXVI: The world is woven all of dream and error   161
Sonnet XXVIII: The edge of the green wave whitely doth hiss   162
Sonnet XXXV: Good. I have done. My heart weighs. I am sad   162

Letters and other writings explaining the heteronyms

"The Genesis of my Heteronyms"   *163*
from "Notes in Memory of My Master Caeiro Signed by Álvaro
de Campos"   *167*
From *Letters to Armando Cortes Rodrigues*   *167*

Some Biographical Dates

169

ERRATA

Page and Line	Should Be
(v), 8	Hello, shepherd
(v), 14	XLVII
(vi), 1	Álvaro
ix, 12	heartbreakingly
ix, 30	temper
x, 19	unexpected
3, 13	saudosismo
3, 25	Negreiros; Carneiro
4, 9	homogeneous
4, 26	contradiction
4, 27	simultaneously
4, 33	by Campos'
4, 36	Negreiros
5, 14	power
5, 33	Secretariat
6, 28	*Oblíqua*
6, 39	de Campos
7, 7	he
7, 10	Vicente
8, 33	Teive
10, 21	in
12, 15	presumably
12, 27	Campos'
12, 40	Larbaud; Negreiros
13, between 6 & 7 insert	to speak: he whistles, he squeaks, he chatters, hammers,
15, footnote 6	(belongs at bottom of page 14)
15, 31	*próprio*
16, 34	Álvaro; Ricardo
17, 1	Portuguese
26, 4	pensamentos
28, 1	importo [title]
28, 7 from end	É
28, 2 from end	E

Page and Line	Should Be
34, poem XLVII, line 2	vontade
35, [poem number]	XLVII
37, first verse, 3	know
38, 7 from end	pensar
46, 1 (title)	outrem
(53)(half-title)	Álvaro
54, 1 (title)	constipaçâo
56, 1	E
58, 11	encontros
61, 20	Álvaro
64, 10	(Deixa-me
64, 11	pescoço . . .)
71, 14	nexus.
72, 3	era eu
72, 11	caco
76, 10	errôneo
76, 5 from end	À
81, 15	Not
82, 16	(Tu,
83, 10	out
84, 10	máscara,
85, 24	Tobacco
85, 29	Shop
86, 5 from end	chegou
91, 8	such a dock
91, after 22 insert	Our docks in our ports,
91, 4 from end	Great Docks
98, 2	metáforas,
98, 11 from end, delete line and insert	E eu, que amo a civilização moderna, eu que beijo com a alma
98, 10 from end	máquinas,
98, 9 from end	estrangeiro,
98, 7 from end	madeira,
99, 11 from end	civilizations,

· Preface

A Note on the Translations

Pessoa's poems lend themselves to a wide range of inventive possibilities in translation. This quality in the original is of course related to the poet's heteronymic schizophrenia. It is a recognized fact that Pessoa was a supreme inventor who made possible new combinations of sophisticated and idiomatic usages way beyond those of his contemporaries or of any Portuguese poet since Camões. Now no poet can write in Portuguese without feeling his influence. And, if Mário António, the Angolese poet, is right, even the chambermaids in Lisbon now speak a different Portuguese from their mothers' because Fernando Pessoa wrote his poems.

All this makes him a heatbreakingly seductive poet to translate. Like Baudelaire and Rilke his work elicits immediate rapport, which by its very nature gradually misleads enthusiasm, defeats confident expectation, and eludes—always eludes—whatever simple or subtle equivalence one creates in order to contain each poem. But some of the oddness that stands out in translation is also fixed in the flesh of the original. Frequently the Portuguese poems of Ricardo Reis and Fernando Pessoa evince the same antiquated turn of phrase with its typical metaphysical shadowing which one finds in Pessoa's highly mannered English sonnets. I have been unable to imagine a way of putting the Portuguese into English without retaining this oddness, the slightly sprained movement and pitch of the Portuguese.

But oddness is not far from awkwardness, and awkwardness is least tolerable in poetic translation, as some of my poet friends who have glanced at these versions quickly reminded me. Well, Donne is odd and awkward too; so is Shakespeare. Also Herbert, Crashaw, Hopkins, Dickinson, and so on and so on. What does one do about it? One learns to tempers one's first impatience with a sense of something unexpected—the precision which Pessoa is thereby expressing, as much through the heteronym's deliberately cultivated voice as through the particularities of the poem itself. What success my versions achieve may finally depend on whether they instigate other translators to try, fumble, fall, and rise again to the immense challenge of all the heteronymic works. One day someone will perhaps put some of them into an English that moves as the poems do in Portuguese, with all their crooked grace and power, as if they were alive.

I have had constant encouragement and strong intermittent support over the past six years from José Palla e Carmo, the Lisbon lawyer, bank manager, literary critic, and subtle interpreter of American poetry. Palla e Carmo first showed me what Pessoa's language was like, and provided me with basic working samples of many of the poems in prose translations.

His aid in re-examining the entire manuscript sometimes amounted to collaboration. Pessoa's first literary English translator, the American poet and polymath, Edouard Roditi, generously went over several stages of the manuscript; his special knowledge in some instances proved decisive. The late Thomas Merton was an unepected source of encouragement. After publishing his group of "Twelve Poems by Alberto Caeiro" in *New Directions Annual 19,* he answered my letter, asking what other Pessoa poems he had translated, with the information that he would do no others and had mainly done the dozen to convince Suzuki that Pessoa had really created a Zen Buddhist in the heteronymic poet, Caeiro.

I acknowledge the permission granted me by Pessoa's heir and half-brother, Sr. Louis Rosa, to publish these translations, and also the permission of Octavio Paz to translate his essay which appeared in the introduction to his volume of Pessoa translations in Spanish, *Antología* (Mexico City, 1962). The Portuguese texts are taken from the authorized eight-volume edition, *Obras Completas de Fernando Pessoa,* Edições Ática (Lisbon, 1963).

E. H.

Introduction
Pessoa or the Imminence of the Unknown[1]
****

He is born in Lisbon in 1888. While still a child, his father dies. His mother remarries; in 1896 he is taken along with his siblings to Durban, South Africa, where her second husband has been sent as Portuguese Consul. An English education. In 1905 Fernando Pessoa returns to Lisbon, just as he completes his secondary-school studies and is about to enter the University at Capetown. A bilingual poet, the Anglo-Saxon influence will be constant in his thought and work. In 1907 he drops his courses in the School of Letters in Lisbon and sets up a print shop. A failure—the word will often recur during his lifetime. Then he works as a "foreign correspondent"—meaning, a sort of journeyman commercial-letter writer in English and French, a modest job that will give him just enough to get along on most of his life. To be sure, once or twice the doors to a university career are opened to him, but he refuses the offer with the pride of the timid. I wrote *discretion* and *pride;* perhaps it would have been better to say *disinclination* and *realism.* In 1932 he tries for the job of archivist in a library and is turned down. But there was no rebelliousness in his life— simply a modesty like disdain.

After returning from Africa he doesn't leave Lisbon again. First he lives in an old house, with his maiden aunt and a mad grandmother; then, with another aunt; at another time with his mother; then, with another aunt; at another time with his mother, widowed again; the rest of the time, in uncertain domiciles. He sees his friends in the streets and in the cafes. A solitary drinker in taverns and bars in the old quarter. Other details. In 1916 he plans to establish himself as an astrologer. * * * In 1920 he falls in love, or thinks de does, with an office girl. The affair doesn't last long: "My destiny," he writes in a letter breaking up the relationship, "belongs to another Law, whose existence you don't even suspect. . . ." There's no record of other liaisons. An undercurrent of unhappy homosexuality runs through the *Maritime Ode* and the *Salutation to Whitman*

[1] I have supplied this title—from a phrase Paz uses at the end of this essay—for the original, "El Desconocido de Sí Mismo," which is untranslatable but which the essay superbly explains. Asterisks indicate that material has been omitted in translation.—E.H.

—great poems that make one think of those García Lorca would write fifteen years later in *Poet in New York*. But Álvaro de Campos, a professional at being provoked, is not the whole Pessoa. There are other poets in Pessoa. Chaste as he is, all his passions are imaginary; better put, his great vice is the imagination. Which is why he doesn't stir out of his chair. And there's another Pessoa who doesn't belong to daily life or to literature: the disciple, the initiate. About this Pessoa nothing can or need be said. Revelation, hoax, self-deception? All together, perhaps. Like the master of one of his hermetic sonnets, Pessoa *knows and says nothing*.

Anglomanic, myopic, courteous, elusive, dressed in black, reticent and familiar, the cosmopolitan who preaches nationalism, *the solemn investigator of useless things,* the humorist who never smiles and makes our blood run cold, the inventor of other poets and self-destroyer, the author of paradoxes clear as water, and like water, dizzying: *to pretend is to know oneself*, the mysterious one who doesn't cultivate mystery, mysterious as the moon at noon, the taciturn ghost of the Portuguese midday—who is Pessoa? Pierre Hourcade, who knew him at the end of his life, writes, "Never, on taking leave of him, did I dare turn around; I was afraid of seeing him vanish, disappear in thin air." Anything else? In 1935 he died of a hepatic colon, in Lisbon. He left two "brochures" of poems in English, a thin booklet of Portuguese verse, and a trunk full of manuscripts. His complete works have not yet been published.

His public life—in some way that's what one must call it—takes place among shadows. A literature made outside himself in the penumbra where they move—conspirators or lunatics?—those indecisive shadows of Álvaro de Campos, Ricardo Reis, and Fernando Pessoa. For an instant startling reflections of scandal and polemic light them up. Then the darkness again. Near-anonymity and near-celebrity. No one is unacquainted with Fernando Pessoa's name, but few know who he is and what he does. Among Portuguese, Spanish, and Latin-American reputations: "The name rings a bell —isn't he a newspaperman or a movie director?" I don't think Pessoa would find the mistake disagreeable. More to the point, it's just what he was always cultivating. Flurries of literary activity followed by spells of doing nothing. If his appearances are isolated and spasmodic, like hand slams to terrorize the four cats of official literature, his solitary work is constant. Like all great idlers, he spent his life making up lists of books he'd never write; and as usual among such idlers when they are passionate and imaginative, in order to keep going and not go mad, they write something daily, almost on the sly, in the margins of their great projects, a poem, an article, a reflection. Fragmentation and tension. But all of it having the same trademark—each thing written by necessity. And this, a fatality, is what distinguishes an authentic writer from a simply talented one.

Between 1905 and 1908 he writes his first poem in English. At that time he was reading Milton, Shelley, Keats, Poe. Later he discovers Baudelaire and takes to a few "Portuguese subpoets." Instinctively he returns to his native language, although he'll never stop writing in English. Until 1912 the influence of Symbolist poetry and *saudismo*[2] is predominant. That year he publishes his first piece in the magazine *A Águia (The Eagle),* literary organ of the "Portuguese Renaissance." His contribution consisted of a series of articles on Portuguese poetry. This sort of thing—beginning his writing career with literary criticism—is very Pessoan. No less significant is the title of one of his pieces, "In the Forest of Estrangement." The theme of alienation and the search for the self, in the enchanted wood or the abstract city, is something more than a subject: it is the substance of his work. In those years he was looking for himself; it was not long before he invented himself.

In 1913 he gets to know two young men who will become his closest associates in the short-lived Futurist adventure: the painter Almada Negreira and the poet Mário de Sá-Caneiro. Other friendships: Armando Côrtes-Rodrigues, Luis de Montalvor, José Pacheco. Still under the spell of "decadent" poetry, these young men try vainly to recapture the Symbolist movement. Pessoa invents "paulism". Then suddenly, through Sá-Carneiro, who lives in Paris and with whom he keeps up a feverish correspondence, comes the discovery of the great modern insurrection: Marinetti. The fertility of Futurism is undeniable, though its brilliance is later obscured by the demurrals of its founder. The repercussions of the movement were instantaneous, perhaps because instead of being a revolution it was a mutiny. It was the first spark, the spark that set off the dynamite. And the fire spread from one extreme to another—from

---

[2] Perhaps best described as a superannuated Portuguese version of French Parnassism, and noted for its cultivation of nostalgic subjects and tonalities, it combines something of Becquer's confirmed uneasiness with the evanescent musicality of Verlaine. (E.H.)

Moscow to Lisbon. Three great poets: Apollinaire, Mayakovski, and Pessoa. For the Portuguese poet the following year, 1914, would be a discovery date or, more exactly, a date of birth: Alberto Caeiro and his disciples appear—Álvaro de Campos and the Neo-classical Ricardo Reis.

The eruption of the heteronyms, an internal event, antecedes the public act: the explosion of *Orpheu*. In April 1915 the first number of the magazine appears; in July, the second and last issue. Negligible? Perhaps too much. The group was not homogenous. The name itself —*Orpheu* (spelt with a *ph*)—makes a point of its Symbolist origin. But the critics note the persistent "decadence," even in Sá-Carneiro, despite his violence. In Pessoa the division is clean-cut: Álvaro de Campos is a full-fledged Futurist while Fernando Pessoa continues to be a "paulist" poet. Public reaction to the magazine was indignation. The pieces by Sá-Carneiro and de Campos provoked the usual outrage from the journalists. First, the insults, then, the jokes; after the jokes, silence. The end of a cycle. Anything left over? In the first number *Triumphal Ode* appeared; in the second, *Maritime Ode*. Despite its tics and affectations, the former is a poem which already has the direct tone of *Tobacco Shop,* the vision of man's insignificance faced with the brutal pressure of social life. The second poem evinces something more than the artificial fireworks of Futurist poetry: a great spirit raving out loud whose cry is never animal or superhuman. The poet is not "a small God," but a fallen creature. Both poems recall Whitman more than Marinetti, a self-preoccupied and nay-saying Whitman. But that's not all. Contradition is its method, the form of its vital coherence. And simultaneous with the two odes, he writes *The Shepherd,* a posthumous work by Alberto Caeiro, as well as the Latinate poems of Reis, and *Epithalamium* and *Antinous*—"two of my English poems, very obscene, and there-fore unpublishable in England."

The Orpheu episode ends abruptly. Under attack from the news-papermen and perhaps put off by de Campos' intemperance, a few sneak away. Sá-Carneiro, always unstable, returns to Paris. A year later he commits suicide. In 1917 a new attempt: the only number of *Portugal Futurista,* headed by Almada Negreira, in which Álvaro de Campos' *Ultimatum* appears. Today it's hard to read that stream of diatribes with any interest, although there's still a healthy viru-lence in a few of them: "D'Annunzio as Don John of Patmos; Shaw

the frozen tumor of Ibsenism; Kipling, imperialist on the bedpan
. . . ." *Orpheu* ends with the group's dispersion and the death of one
of its leaders. Fifteen years will go by before there's a new generation.
Nothing unusual about that. The astonishing thing is that the group
appeared at all, way ahead of its time and the social temper. What
was being written in Spain and Latin America during those years?

The next period is one of relative obscurity. Pessoa publishes his
two pamphlets of English poetry, *35 Sonnets* and *Antinous,* to which
the *London Times* and *Glasgow Herald* respond courteously and
tepidly. In 1922 appears "The Anarchist Banker," Pessoa's first con-
tribution to *Contemporânia,* a new literary magazine. These are also
the years of his political velleities: eulogies to nationalism and the au-
thoritarian regime. Reality disillusions him and forces him to turn the
tables on himself: on two occasions he confronts public popwer, the
Church and social morality. The first time to defend Antonio Botto,
author of *Songs,* poems of homosexual love. The next time against
the League of Student Action, which was persecuting free-thought
under the pretext of destroying the so-called "literature of Sodom."
Caesar is always a moralist. Álvaro de Campos distributes a leaflet,
"Warning About Morality"; Pessoa publishes a manifesto, and the
aggrieved Raúl Leal writes a pamphlet, *A Moral Lesson for the
Students of Lisbon and the Impudence of the Catholic Church.* The
center of gravity shifts from free art to the freedom of art. The
nature of our society is such that the creator is forced into hetero-
doxy and opposition. The clearminded artist does not shirk the
moral risk involved.

In 1924, a new magazine, *Atena.* It lasts only five issues. Warmed-
over dishes are never any good. Actually, *Atena* is a bridge between
Orpheu and the young men around *Presença* (1927). As it appears
each generation chooses its own tradition. The new group discovers
Pessoa: he finally meets interlocutors. Too late, as always. Not much
afterward, a year before his death, there's the grotesque incident of
the poetry contest sponsored by the Secretary of National Informa-
tion. The theme, of course, was a panegyric to the glories of nation
and empire. Pessoa sent *Mensagem (Messages),* a group of poems
that are an "occult" and symbolic interpretation of Portuguese
history. The collection must have puzzled the functionaries respon-
sible for the contest. They gave him a second prize. This was his last
literary experience.

It all begins on March 8, 1914. But it is better to quote part of Pessoa's letter to Adolfo Casais Monteiro, one of the young men at *Presença:*

> Some time around 1912, unless I'm mistaken (which couldn't be by very much), the idea came to me to write some poems of pagan character. I tried sketching some things in free verse (not in the style of Álvaro de Campos but in my own normal style), and then abandoned the attempt. But in the dim confusion I made out the hazy outline of the person that was writing. (Without my knowing it, Ricardo Reis had been born.) A year and a half or two years later, I remember one day taking up Sá-Carneiro's challenge to invent a bucolic poet, of a complicated sort, and present him, I don't recall now how, as if he were really a living creature. I spent a few days working on him without getting anywhere. One day, just as I'd finally given up —it was March 8, 1914—I went over to a high desk, and taking a piece of paper, began to write, standing up, as I always do when possible. And I wrote some thirty poems, one after another, in a sort of ecstasy, the nature of which I'm unable to define. It was the triumphant day of my life, and never will there be another like it. I began with the title, *The Shepherd.* What followed was the appearance in me of someone to whom I immediately gave the name of Alberto Caeiro. Forgive me the absurdity of the sentence: in me there appeared my master. That was my immediate reaction. So much so that, scarcely were those thirty odd poems written when I took fresh paper and wrote, again without stopping, the six poems constituting *Chuva Obliqua (Oblique Rain),* by Fernando Pessoa. Straight off and fully formed . . . It was the return of Fernando Pessoa-Alberto Caeiro to Fernando Pessoa himself. Or, better, it was the reaction of Fernando Pessoa to his nonexistence as Alberto Caeiro. Once Alberto Caeiro had appeared I instinctively and subconsciously tried to find disciples for him. Out of him I plucked the false paganism latent in Ricardo Reis, I discovered the name and adapted it to him, since I'd already seen him at that level. And suddenly, derived from and opposed to Ricardo Reis, there impetuously arose in me a new individual. At once, and on the typewriter, there surged up, without interruption or correction, the *Triumphal Ode* of Álvaro do Campos—the ode so entitled together with the man so named.

I don't know what there is to add to this confession.

Psychology offers a variety of explanations. Pessoa himself, who was interested in his own case, proposes two or three. One crudely pathological: "I'm probably an hysterico-neurasthenic . . . and this explains, more or less, the organic origin of the heteronyms." I'd say "less" rather than "more." The trouble with these hypotheses is not that they're false but that they're incomplete. A neurotic is an obsessive. But if he controls his disturbance, is he sick? The neurotic suffers his obsessions; the creative person masters and transforms them. Pessoa tells of living with imaginary people from the time has was a child. ("I don't know, of course, if it was they who didn't exist or if it was I who didn't: in such instances one shouldn't be dogmatic.") The heteronyms are surrounded by a fluid mass of semi-beings: Bernardo Soares, ghost of the ghostly Vincente Guedos; Pacheco, a poor copy of Campos. . . . Not all of them are writers. There's a Mr. Cross, the indefatigable contributor to charades and crossword-puzzle contests in the English magazines (an infallible means, according to Pessoa, of getting rid of the blues), Alexander Search, and others. All this—like his solitude, his discrete alcoholism, and other things—gives us hints about his personality but tells us nothing about his poems, which is the only thing that really matters to us.

The same is true of the so-called "occultist," whom Pessoa, being overly analytical, doesn't openly admit but never stops evoking. It's a well-known fact that spirits who guide the pen of mediums, whether of Euripides or of Victor Hugo, show a disconcerting literary torpor. Others believe this to be a matter of "mystification." The error is doubly vulgar: Pessoa is neither a liar nor is his work a fraud. There's something terribly mean-spirited about the modern mind. People who tolerate all sorts of debased falsehoods in real life and swallow every kind of worthless fact, won't accept the existence of the fable. And that's what Pessoa's work is: a fable, a fiction. To forget that Caeiro, Reis, and Campos are poetic creations is forgetting too much. Like every creation these poets are born out of play. Art is play—among other things. But there is no art without play.

The authenticity of the heteronyms depends on its poetic coherence, its verisimilitude. They were necessary creations because in no other way could Pessoa have devoted his life to living and creating them; what counts now is not that they were necessary for their author but that they are also necessary for us. Pessoa, their first reader, did not doubt their reality. Reis and Campos told what he perhaps would never tell. In contradicting him they expressed him;

in expressing him they made him invent himself. We write to be what we are or to be what we aren't. In either case we are looking for ourselves. And if we are lucky enough to find ourselves—the sign of creation—we'll discover that we are an unknown person. Always the other, always he, inseparable, alien, having your face and mine, you who are always with me and always alone.

The heteronyms are not literary masks: "What Fernando Pessoa writes belongs to two kinds of works; we might call them orthonyms and heteronyms. We can't say they're anonyms or pseudonyms, because they aren't really. The pseudonymous work is by the author in his own person, except that he uses another name; the heteronymous is by the author outside his own person. . . ." Gérard de Nerval is the pseudonym for Gérard Labrunie: same person, same work. Caeiro is a heteronym of Pessoa's; impossible to confuse the two. Closer to home, the case of Antonio Machado is also different. Abel Martín and Juan de Mairena are not entirely the poet Antonio Machado. They are masks, but transparent masks; a piece by Machado is not distinct from one by Mairena. Also, Machado is not possessed by his fiction, they are not creatures he lives inside of, who contradict or deny him. Caeiro, Reis, and Campos, on the other hand, are the heroes of a novel which Pessoa never wrote. "I am a dramatic poet," he confided in a letter to J. G. Simões. Nevertheless, the relationship between Pessoa and his heteronyms is not the same as that between the dramatist or the novelist and his characters. He is not an inventor of poet characters but a creator of poet works. The distinction is crucial. As Casais Monteiro says, "He invented the biographies for the sake of the works and not the works for the sake of the biographies." Those works—including the poems by Pessoa written facing them, by means of as well as against them—are his poetic work. He himself turns into one of the works in his work. And not even he has the privilege of being the critic of this coterie. Reis and Campos treat him with a certain condescension; Baron de Tieve does not always greet him; Vicente, the archivist, resembles him so much that when they meet, in some neighborhood eating-place, he feels a twinge of pity for himself. He is the bewitched enchanter, so totally possessed by his phantasmagorias that he feels them watching him, perhaps scornfully, perhaps sympathetically. Our creations do judge us.

"Alberto Caeiro is my master." This affirmation is the touchstone of all his work. And to this may be added that Caeiro's work is the only affirmation that Pessoa made. Caeiro is the sun in whose orbit Reis, Campos, and Pessoa himself rotate. In each are particles of negation or unreality: Reis believes in form, Campos in sensation, Pessoa in symbols. Caeiro doesn't believe in anything: he exists. The sun is life that is full of itself; the sun shines not because its rays are glances converted into heat and light; the sun is not aware of itself because for the sun thinking and being are one and the same thing. Caeiro is everything that Pessoa is not, and more—everything a modern poet could never be: a man reconciled to nature. Before Christianity, yes, but also before work and history. Before consciousness. Caeiro denies, by the mere act of existing, not just the Symbolist esthetic of Pessoa but all esthetics, all values, all ideas. Does nothing remain? Everything remains, clean of ghosts and the cobwebs of culture. The world exists because my senses tell me so; and by so telling me they tell me I too exist. Yes, I shall die and the world will die, but to die is to live. Caeiro's affirmation annuls death; by overcoming consciousness it overcomes nothingness. It doesn't affirm that everything is, since that would be to affirm an idea. It says that everything exists. And even more—it says only that is which exists. The rest are illusions. Campos sees to it that the *i* is dotted. "My master Caeiro was not a pagan; he was paganism." I would add, an idea of paganism.

Caeiro scarcely went to school. When he heard himself called a "materialist poet" he wanted to know what the doctrine was all about. When Campos explained it to him, he couldn't keep his surprise to himself. "That's a notion of priests without religion! You mean to say they say space is infinite? What space have they been looking at?" To his disciple's stupefaction, Caeiro maintained that space is finite. "What has no limits doesn't exist. . . ." The other replied, "Well, what about numbers? After 34 there's 35, then 36, and so on, consecutively. . . ." Caeiro stood there looking at him pitifully: "But those are *only* numbers!" adding, with crushing childlikeness, "Is there really in fact a number 34?" Another anecdote: they asked him, "Are you happy with yourself?" And he answered, "No, I am happy." Caeiro is not a philosopher: he's a sage. Thinkers have ideas; for the sage, living and thinking are not separate acts. For that reason it's impossible to express the ideas of Socrates and Lao Tse. They did not leave doctrines but a handful of anecdotes, enigmas and poems. Chuang Tse, more faithful than Plato, does not try to give us a philosophy but to tell us little stories; philosophy is inseparable from the story. It is story. The philosopher's doctrine incites refutation; the life of the sage is irrefutable. No sage proclaims that you can learn truth; what they all—or almost all of them—say is that the only truth worth bothering to live for is to experience truth. Caeiro's weakness is not in his ideas (actually, that's his strength); it's in the unreality of the experience he claims to be embodying.

Adam in some corner of a Portuguese province, with no wife, no children, and no antecedent; he has no consciousness, no job, no religion. One sensation among other sensations, one existence among other existences. The stone's a stone and Caeiro's Caeiro—for the moment. Later, each will be something else. Or the same thing. It's the same or it's different: everything is the same through being different. To be named is to be. The word for stone is not the stone but has the same reality as the stone. Caeiro does not propose giving beings any name, and so he never tells us whether the stone is an agate or a cobblestone, if the tree is a pine or an oak. Nor does he hope to set up relations among things; the word *like* doesn't figure in his vocabulary; everything is submerged it its own reality. If Caeiro speaks it's because man is a word-using animal, as the bird is a wing-using animal. Man speaks the way the river runs or the rain falls. The innocent poet doesn't have to name things; his words are trees, clouds, spiders, lizards. Not those spiders I see but these that I speak of. The idea that reality is ungraspable astonishes Caeiro: here it is, in front of us; touching it is enough. Speaking is enough.

It wouldn't be hard to demonstrate to Caeiro that reality is never graspable and that we must conquer it (though at the risk of its evaporating before us in the act, or of its being changed into something else—an idea, a tool). The innocent poet is a myth, but a myth that is the basis of poetry. The real poet knows words and things are not the same, and so in order to re-establish a precarious unity between man and the world, he names things with his images, rhythms, symbols, and comparisons. Words are not things; they are the bridges we set up between ourselves and them. The poet is the consciousness of words—that is, the nostalgia for the *real* reality of things. Words of course were also things before they became the names for things. This is what they were in the myth of the innocent poet, that is, before language. The opaque words of the real poet evoke speech prior to language, the scarcely glimpsed paradisaical covenant. Innocent speech: silence in which nothing is said because everything has been said, everything is bespeaking itself. The poet's language feeds on this silence, which is innocent speech. Pessoa, a real poet and a skeptical man, had to invent an innocent poet in order to justify his own poetry. Reis, Campos, and Pessoa speak mortal and dated words, words of loss and fragmentation; they are the presentiment of the nostalgia for unity. We hear them against the backdrop of the silence of that unity. It is no accident that Caeiro should die young, before his disciples begin their work. He is their foundation, the silence which sustains them.

The most natural and simplest of the heteronyms is the least real. Because of the excess of reality. Man, especially modern man, is not all real. He is not a compact entity like nature or things; his self-consciousness is his unsubstantial reality. Caeiro is an absolute affirmation of existence, whence his words appear to us to be truths from another time, a time when everything was one and the same. A sensate, untouchable presence: as we name it, it evaporates! The mask of innocence Caeiro turns on us is not wisdom: to be wise is to resign ourselves to knowing we are not innocent. Pessoa, who knows this, is closer to wisdom.

The other extreme is Álvaro de Campos.[3] Caeiro lives in the timeless present of children and animals; the Futurist Campos, in the moment. For the former, his village is the center of the world; the other, a cosmopolitan, has no center, and is exiled in that no-man's-land which is everywhere. Yet they resemble one another: they both cultivate free verse; they both do violence to the Portuguese language; neither is afraid of being prosaic. They do not believe in anything they cannot touch, they're pessimists, love concrete reality, don't love their fellow creatures, scorn ideas, and live outside of history—one in the plenitude of being, the other in extremest privation. Caeiro, the innocent poet, is what Pessoa couldn't be; Campos, the vagabond dandy, is what he could have

[3] Born in Tavira, October 15, 1890. The date coincides with his horoscope, says Pessoa. High school studies, then naval engineering in Glasgow. Of Jewish stock. Voyages to the Orient. Artificial paradises and so forth. A proponent of non-Aristotelian esthetics he sees fulfilled by three poets: Whitman, Caeiro, and himself. He wore a monocle. An impassive, irascible man.

been and wasn't. They are the vital, impossible possibilities of Pessoa.

Campos's first poem has a deceptive originality. *Triumphal Ode* is apparently a brilliant echo of Whitman and the Futurists. One can hardly compare the poem with those being written at the time in France, Russia, and other countries, before noticing the differences.[4] Whitman really believed in man and machines; better yet, he believed that *natural man* was not incompatible with machines. His pantheism also welcomed industry. Most of his descendants do not agree with such illusions. Some see the machine as a marvelous plaything. I'm thinking of Valéry Larbaud and his Barnabooth, who resembles Álvaro de Campos[5] in more ways than one. Larbaud's attitude toward the machine is Epicurean; that of the Futurists, visionary. They see it as the destructive agent of false humanism and, presumbaly, of *natural man*. They don't suggest humanizing the machine but constructing a new human species like it. An exception to this would be Mayakovski, and even he . . . *Triumphal Ode* is neither romantic nor Epicurean nor triumphant; it is a song of hate and defeat. And this is the basis of its originality.

A factory is a "tropical landscape" populated by huge, lascivious beasts. Endless fornication of wheels, pistons and pulleys. As the mechanical rhythm speeds up the paradise of iron and electricity turns into a torture chamber. The machines are the sexual organs of destruction: Campos would like to be torn to pieces by their furious helices. This strange vision is less fantastic than it seems and is not an obsession of Campo's alone. Machines are the reproduction, simplification, and multiplication of vital processes. They seduce and horrify us because they give us the

[4] There was no one like him in Spanish till Lorca's and Neruda's generation. Yes, there was the prose written by the great Ramón Gómez de la Serna. In Mexico we had a modest beginning, but only a beginning, in Tablada. 1918 was when modern poetry really opened up in Spanish. But its initiator, Vicente Huidobro, is a poet of a very different cast.

[5] It seems to me almost impossible that Pessoa should not have known Larbaud's book. The definitive edition of Barnabooth was issued in 1913, a year of intensive correspondence with Sá-Carneiro. A curious detail: Larbaud visited Lisbon in 1926; Gómez de la Serna, who lived there then, introduced him to the young writers, who gave him a banquet. In the journal entry he devotes to this event (*Lisbon Letter*, in *Yellow Blue White*) Larboud praises Almada Negreira but doesn't mention Pessoa. Did they know of one another?

feeling of intelligence and unconsciousness simultaneously; every-
thing they do they do well, but they don't know what they're
doing. Isn't this the image of modern man? But machines are
one facet of contemporary civilization. The other is social promis-
cuity. *Triumphal Ode* ends in a scream; transformed into a bulk,
a box, a package, a wheel, Álvaro de Campos loses the capacity
explodes. Caeiro's word evokes the unity of man, stone, and
insect; that of Campos, the incoherent noise of history. Pantheism
and pan-machinism, two means of abolishing the consciousness.

Tobacco Shop is the poem of recovered consciousness. Caeiro
asks himself, "What am I?" Campos, "Who am I?" From his
room he studies the street: automobiles, passers-by, dogs, all real
and all hollow, all of them close by and all of them far away.
Across the way, sure of himself as a god, enigmatic and smiling
like a god, rubbing his hands like God Almighty after his horrible
creation, the Owner of the Tobacco Shop appears and disappears.
Arriving at his combination lair-temple-shop is Stevens, the indif-
ferent one, who speaks and eats "without metaphysics," has feel-
ings and political opinions, and keeps the holy days of obligation.
From his window—his consciousness—, Campos looks out at the
two puppets and seeing them sees himself. Where is reality—in
me or in Stevens? The Tobacco Shop Owner smiles and does not
answer. Campos, the Futurist poet, begins by affirming that the
only reality is sensation; a few years later he asks himself if he
himself has any reality.

In abolishing his self-consciousness Caeiro eliminates history;
but it is history that suppresses Campos. Marginal life: his brothers,
if he has any, are the prostitutes, bums, dandies, beggars, the
scum of high and low societies. His rebellion has no place at all
for ideas of redemption or justice: "No, anything but being right!
Anything but caring about humanity! Anything rather than give
in to humanitarianism!" Campos rebels against the idea of rebel-
lion too. It's not a moral virtue, a state of consciousness—it's the
consciousness of a sensation: "Ricardo Reis is a pagan by con-
viction; Antonio Mora, by intelligence; I am one by rebellion,
that is, by temperament." His sympathy for shady characters is
mixed with contempt, but it's a contempt he feels for himself
above all:

I feel for all those people,
Especially when they don't deserve it.
Yes, I'm also a drifter and a sponger . . .
Being lazy and a beggar isn't being lazy and a beggar:
It's being outside the social hierarchy . . .
It's not being a Supreme Court Judge, a full-time worker,
    a prostitute,
Down and out, exploited proletarian,
Somebody with an incurable disease,
Hungry for Justice, or a captain in the cavalry,
It's not being, finally, one of those social characters
    invented by novelists
Bored stiff with literature because they've every right
    to pour on the tears
And rebelling against society because they've got more than
    enough reason to do so . . .

His vagrancy and beggarliness don't depend on any particular circumstance; they're incurable and unredeemable. To be vagrant that way is *to be isolated in one's soul.* And further, with a brutality that scandalized Pessoa: "I don't even have the excuse of being able to have social opinions . . . I'm clear-headed. None of your damned humane esthetics: I'm clear. Shit! I'm clear-headed!"

The consciousness of exile has been a constant note in modern society for a century and a half. Gérard de Nerval pretends to be the Prince of Aquitaine; Álvaro de Campos chooses the mask of the vagrant. The shift is revealing. Troubadour or beggar— what hides behind the mask? Nothing, maybe. The poet is the consciousness of his historical unreality. Only if that consciousness withdraws from history, society founders in its own opaque abyss, turns into Stevens or the Tobacco Shop Owner. There's no lack of people to say that Campos' attitude is not "positive." To critics of this sort, Casais Monteiro replied, "Pessoa's work is *really* a negative work. It's not a model, it doesn't teach you to handle others or be handled. It's useful because it does just the opposite: it undisciplines the spirit."

Campos doesn't rush ahead, like Caeiro, to become everything, but to be everyone and everywhere. The drop into plurality is paid for by the loss of one's identity. Ricardo Reis selects the other latent possibility in his master's poetry.[6] Reis is a hermit as Campos is a vagabond. His hermitage is a philosophy and a form. The philosophy is a mixture of Stoicism and Epicureanism.

The form, the epigram, the ode, and the elegy of the Neoclassical poets. Except that the Neoclassicism is a nostalgia, which is to say, a romanticism that either is unaware of itself or that disguises itself. While Campos writes his long monologues that come closer to being introspections than hymns, his friend Reis polishes little odes on pleasure, the flight of time, the roses of Lydia, the illusory freedom of man, the vanity of the gods. Educated in a Jesuit school, a doctor by profession, a monarchist, exiled in Brazil since 1919, a pagan and skeptic by conviction, a Latinist by education, Reis lives outside of time. He seems to be, but is not, a man out of the past. He has chosen to live in a timeless *sagesse*. Cioran recently indicated that our century, which has invented so many things, has not created what is needed most. It is not surprising that some find it in Oriental tradition: Taoism, Zen Buddhism. Actually, those doctrines serve the same function that the moral philosophies of the classical period did. Reis's Stoicism is a manner of not being in the world, without actually leaving it. His political ideas have a similar significance: they are not a program but a negation of the present state of things. He neither hates Christ nor does he love Him: he abhors Christianity, although—esthete to the end—when he thinks of Jesus he admits that "his pitiful suffering form brought us something that was missing." The true deity for Reis is Fate, and all of us, men and myths, are subject to its rule.

The form Reis uses, like all artificial perfection, is admirable and monotonous. One sees in those little poems, more than his familiarity with the Latin and Greek originals, a wise and distilled mixture of Lusitanian Neoclassicism and the Greek Anthology translated into English. The correctness of his language disturbs Pessoa: "Caeiro writes Portuguese poorly; Campos does a reasonable job of it, though he falls into saying such things as *eu própio* for *eu mesmo;* Reis writes better than I but with a purity which I consider exaggerated." The somnambulist exaggeration of

---

[6] He was born in Oporto in 1887. He is the most Mediterranean of the heteronyms: Caeiro was blond with blue eyes; Campos "between light and dark," tall, thin, and having the appearance of a cosmopolitan. Reis is closer to the Spanish and Portuguese meridionial type. The *Odes* are not his only work. He is known to have written an *Esthetic Debate between Ricardo Reis and Alvaro de Campos*. His critical notes on Caeiro and Campos are a model of verbal precision and esthetic incomprehension.

Campos is transformed by an altogether natural movement of contradiction into the exaggerated precision of Reis.

Neither form nor philosophy protects Reis; they protect a phantom. The truth is that Reis doesn't exist and he knows it. Brilliant, with a sharpness more penetrating than Campos' exasperation, he contemplates himself:

> I do not know whose past I recall in me,
> Since I was someone else then, nor do I recognize myself
> When with my heart I feel that other heart
> Which I remember I once felt.
> We forsake ourselves from one day to the next.
> Nothing truly ties us to ourselves—
> We are who we are, and who we were
> Is something we once glimpsed within.

The labyrinth in which Reis loses himself is that of his own self. The poet's looking-inward, something very different from introspection, brings him close to Pessoa. Though both use meters and fixed forms, it is not traditionalism that unites them because they belong to different traditions. The sense of time unites them— not as something which passes before us but as something that becomes us. Prisoners of the moment, Caeiro and Campos affirm being or absence of being in one decisive stroke. Reis and Pessoa lose themselves in the byways of their thought, catch up with themselves at a turn in the path and, fusing with themselves, embrace a shadow. The poem is not the expression of being but the commemoration of that moment of fusion. A hollow monument: Pessoa builds a temple to the unknown; Reis, soberer, writes an epigram that is also an epitaph:

> Let luck deny me everything
> Except to glimpse its workings,
> For I, who am a Stoic but not obdurate,
> Would see the sentence Destiny engraves,
> And letter by letter savor it.

Alvaro de Campos would cite a remark of Richardo Reis': "I hate lying because it is not exact." The words could be applied to Pessoa, so long as you don't confuse lying with imagination or exactness with inflexibility. Reis' poetry is precise and simple as a line drawing; Pessoa's, exact and complex as music. Complex and various, it moves in distinct directions: towards prose, towards poetry in Portugese, and towards poetry in English (one must discount the poems in French as trivial.) The prose pieces, though all are not as yet published, can be divided into two big categories: those appearing over his name and those over his pseudonyms, mainly the Baron de Teive, a decayed aristocrat, and Bernardo Soares, a commercial clerk. In various passages Pessoa stresses that they are not heteronyms: "both write in a style that, for better or worse, is my own. . . ." It's not indispensable to linger over the English poems; their interest is literary and psychological, but they don't amount to much, it seems to me, as English poetry. The poetry in Portuguese, from 1902 to 1935, comprises *Mensagem,* the lyrical poetry, and the dramatic poems. The latter, in my opinion, have a marginal value. Even if they're put to one side, there remains an extensive poetic production. A primary distinction: the heteronyms write in one direction and on one temporal level; only Pessoa splits up like a delta with each arm giving us the image, the whole imagery, of a single moment.

The lyrical poetry branches out into *Mensagem,* the *Cancioneiro (Book of Ballads)* (with its unedited and scattered parts) and the hermetic poems. As usual, the classification doesn't correspond to reality. The *Cancioneiro* is a symbolist book and is impregnated with hermeticism, though the poet doesn't expressly resort to the imagery of the occult tradition. *Mensagem* is, above all, a book of heraldry—and heraldry is part of alchemy. Finally, the hermetic poems are symbolist in form and spirit; one does not have to be an initiate to get into them, nor does understanding them poetically require special knowledge. These poems, like the rest of his work, ask instead for spiritual understanding, the highest and most difficult there is. To know Rimbaud was interested in the Cabbala and identified poetry with alchemy is useful and brings us close to his work; but really to penetrate it one needs something more and something less. Pessoa defines that something else as sympathy, intuition, intelligence, comprehension, and—the most difficult— grace. Perhaps this list seems excessive. I don't see how, though, without these five conditions, one can read Baudelaire, Coleridge or Yeats. In any event, the difficulties of Pessoa's poetry are fewer than those of Hölderlin, Nerval, Mallarmé. . . . In all the poets of the modern tradition poetry becomes a system of analogies and symbols that parallels that of the hermetic sciences. Parallels but is not identical to: the poem is a constellation of signs with light of their own.

Pessoa conceived of *Mensagem* as a ritual; or, say, as an esoteric book. If one is looking for external perfection, it's his most complete book. But it's a contrived book, by which I don't mean that it's insincere but that it's born of the poet's speculations and not his intuitions. At first glace, it is a hymn of glory to Portugal and a prophecy of a new Empire (the Fifth) that will be not a matter of substance but of the spirit; its dominions will extend beyond historical space and time (any Mexican reader at once recalls Vasconcelos' "cosmic race.") The book is a gallery of historical and legendary characters, displaced by traditional reality and transformed into allegories of another tradition and of another reality. Without fully knowing what he was doing, perhaps, Pessoa violated the history of Portugal and, in its stead, presented another, purely spiritual, which is its negation. The esoteric character of *Mensagem* keeps us from reading it as a simple patriotic poem, as some official critics would like to do. One must add that its symbolism does not redeem it. For symbols to work effectively they must stop symbolizing and become palpable, live creatures, not be emblems out of a museum. As in all work where the will intervenes more than inspiration, few poems in *Mensagem* reach the state of grace that distinguishes poetry from *belles lettres*. But those few live in the very magical space of the better poems in *Cancioneiro,* side by side with some of the hermetic sonnets. It is impossible to define what this space consists of; for me it is poetry, properly speaking, its real, tangible territory, which *another* light illuminates. It doesn't matter that they are so few. Benn said: "Nobody, not even the greatest poets of our age, have left more than eight or ten perfect poems .... For six poems, thirty or fifty years of asceticism, of suffering, of fighting!"

The *Cancioneiro,* a work containing few creatures and many shadows. No women, the central sun. Without women the sensuous universe vanishes, there is no terra firma, no water, no incarnation of the impalpable. The terrible pleasures are missing, and also the prohibited ones. Also missing is passion, that love which is desire for a unique being, whoever it may be. There is a vague sentiment of fraternity with nature: trees, clouds, stones, everything fleeting, everything suspended in a temporal vacuum. The unreality of things, reflecting our unreality. There is negation, weariness and disconsolateness. In the *Livro do Desassossêgo (Book of Disquietude),* of which only fragments are known, Pessoa describes his moral landscape: I belong to a generation without faith in Christianity, and which stopped having faith in all other beliefs; we were not enthusiasts of social equality, of beauty or progress; we did not look to the East or the West for other religious forms ("every civilization has an affiliation with the religion that represents it; on losing ours, we lost them all"); a few among us devoted themselves to conquering the quotidian; others, of nobler stock, abstained from public activity, seeking nothing and desiring nothing; still others got interested in the cult of confusion and noise; they thought they were alive when they listened, they thought they were in love when they bumbled up against the externals of love; others of us, "in the End-Race, spiritual limit of the Dead Hour," live in negation, hopeless unhappy. This is not a portrait of Pessoa but certainly of ackground from which his figure stands out and with which confused at times. "Spiritual limit of the Dead Hour": the ₚₒₑₜ is a hollow man who in his helplessness creates a world in order to discover his true identity. All Pessoa's work is a search for lost identity.

In one of his most quoted poems he says that "The poet is a faker. He/ Fakes it so completely,/ He even fakes he's suffering/ The pain he's really feeling." In telling the truth, he lies; in lying, he tells it. We are not dealing with an esthetic but with an act of faith. Poetry is the revelation of its unreality.

> Between the moonlight and the foliage,
> Between the stillness and the grove,
> Between night's being and the breeze,
> A secret passes.
> My soul follows as it passes.

That which passes—is it Pessoa or another? The question repeats itself all through the years and through the poems. He doesn't know if what he writes is his own. Or rather: he knows that though it may be, it isn't: "Why do I, who've been deceived, judge that mine which is mine?" The search for the self—lost and found and lost again—ends in loathing: "Nausea, the will to nothingness: existing not to die."

Only from this perspective can one perceive the full meaning of the heteronyms. They are a literary invention and a psychological necessity but also something more. In a certain way they are what Pessoa might have been or would have liked to be; in another, more profound sense, what he didn't wish to be: a personality. In the first instance, they make a tabula rasa of the idealism and intellectual convictions of their author; in the second, they show that innocent *sagesse,* public square, and hermetic philosophy are all illusions. The moment is uninhabitable, like the future; and stoicism is a remedy which kills. Nevertheless, the destruction of the self, which is what the heteronyms stand for, provokes a secret fertility. The true desert is the Self and not only because it encloses us in ourselves and thus condemns us to live with a ghost, but also because it withers everything it touches. Pessoa's experience, perhaps without his having himself intended it so, fits into the tradition of the great poets of the modern era, from Nerval and the German romantics on. The *I* is an obstacle, *the* obstacle. Which is why any merely esthetic judgment of his work is insufficient. If it is true that not everything he wrote has the same quality, all or almost all of it is marked by the traces of his quest. His work is a step toward the unknown. A passion.

Pessoa's world is neither this world nor the other. The word *absence* would define it, if by absence one understands a fluid state in which presence vanishes and absence heralds what?—a moment in which the present no longer exists and is encroaching on one which perhaps is hardly even dawning. The urban desert is covered with signs: stones say something, the wind speaks, the lighted window and the lone tree on the corner speak; everything is saying something, not the thing I'm saying but something else, always the same something else that is never spoken. Absence is not only privation but the presentiment of a presence that never shows itself entirely. Hermetic poems and songs coincide: in absence, in the unreality that we are, something is present. Astonished among people and things, the poet walks down a street in the old quarter. He enters a park and the leaves are trembling. They are about to say. . . . No, they've said nothing. Unreality of the world, in the last light of the afternoon. Everything is immobile, expectant. The poet already knows that he has no identity. Like those houses, half gilt, half real, like those trees suspended in the hour, he also takes leave of himself. And the other does not appear, the double, the true Pessoa. He will never appear: there is no other. It appears, it insinuates itself, the other, something that has no name, that is not spoken and that our poor words invoke. Is it poetry? No: poetry is what remains and what consoles us, the consciousness of absence. And again, almost imperceptible, a sound of something: Pessoa or the imminence of the unknown.

Octavio Paz
(translated by Edwin Honig)

1

Alberto Caeiro

II. O meu olhar é nítido como um girassol

O meu olhar é nítido como um girassol.
Tenho o costume de andar pelas estradas
Olhando para a direita e para a esquerda,
E de vez em quando olhando para trás . . .
E o que vejo a cada momento
É aquilo que nunca antes eu tinha visto,
E eu sei dar por isso muito bem . . .
Sei ter o pasmo essencial
Que tem uma criança se, ao nascer,
Reparasse que nascera deveras . . .
Sinto-me nascido a cada momento
Para a eterna novidade do Mundo . . .

Creio no mundo como num malmequer,
Porque o vejo. Mas não penso nele
Porque pensar é não compreender . . .
O Mundo não se fez para pensarmos nele
(Pensar é estar doente dos olhos)
Mas para olharmos para ele e estarmos de acordo . . .

Eu não tenho filosofia: tenho sentidos . . .
Se falo na Natureza não é porque saiba o que ela é,
Mas porque a amo, e amo-a por isso,
Porque quem ama nunca sabe a que ama . . .
Nem sabe porque ama, nem o que é amar . . .

Amar é a eterna inocência,
E a única inocência é não pensar . . .

from *The Shepherd*

II. My glance is as clear as a sunflower

My glance is as clear as a sunflower.
I usually take to the roads,
Looking to my right and to my left,
And now and then looking behind me . . .
And what I see each moment
Is something I've never seen before,
And I know very well how to give myself up to it . . .
I know how to feel the same essential wonder
That an infant feels on being born,
Supposing he could know he was being born . . .
I feel that I am being born each moment
Into the eternal newness of the World . . .

I believe in the world as in a daisy,
Because I see it. But I don't think about it,
Because thinking is not understanding . . .
The world was not made for us to think about
(To think is to be sick in the eyes)
But to be looked at and accepted.

I have no philosophy: I have my senses . . .
If I speak of Nature, it's not because I know what Nature is
But becouse I love it, and love it only for that reason,
For a lover never knows what he loves
Nor why he loves, nor what love is . . .

Loving is eternal innocence
And the only innocence is not thinking . . .

IX. Sou um guardador de rebanhos

Sou um guardador de rebanhos.
O rebanho é os meus pensamentos
E os meus pesamentos são todos sensações.
Penso com os olhos e com os ouvidos
E com as mãos e os pés
E com o nariz e a boca.

Pensar uma flor é vê-la e cheirá-la
E comer um fruto é saber-lhe o sentido.

Por isso quando num dia de calor
Me sinto triste de gozá-lo tanto,
E me deito ao comprido na erva,
E fecho os olhos quentes,
Sinto todo o meu corpo deitado na realidade,
Sei a verdade e sou feliz.

X. "Olá, guardador de rebanhos"

«Olá, guardador de rebanhos
Aí à beira da estrada,
Que te diz o vento que passa?»

«Que é vento, e que passa,
E que já passou antes,
E que passará depois.
E a ti o que te diz?»

«Muita coisa mais do que isso,
Fala-me de muitas outras coisas.
De memórias e de saudades
E de coisas que nunca foram».

«Nunca ouviste passar o vento.
O vento só fala do vento.
O que lhe ouviste foi mentira,
E a mentira está em ti».

IX. I'm a shepherd

I'm a shepherd.
My sheep are my thoughts,
And my thoughts are all sensations.
I think with my eyes and ears
And with my hands and feet
And with my nose and mouth.

To think of a flower is to see it and smell it.
And to eat a fruit is to taste its meaning.

And so on a warm day,
When I ache from enjoying it so much,
And stretch out on the grass,
Closing my warm eyes,
I feel my whole body lying full-length in reality,
I know the truth and I'm happy.

X. Hello, shepherd

"Hello, shepherd,
You there, by the roadside,
What does the passing wind tell you?"

"That it's the wind and it blows,
That it's blown before,
And that it'll blow again.
What does it tell you?"

"A great deal more than that.
It speaks to me of many other things.
Of memories and sorrows
And things that never were."

"You've never listened to the wind.
The wind speaks only of the wind.
What you heard in it was a lie,
And that lie is part of you."

XIV. Não me importa com as rimas

Não me importo com as rimas. Raras vezes
Há duas árvores iguais, uma ao lado da outra.
Penso e escrevo como as flores têm cor
Mas com menos perfeição no meu modo de exprimir-me
Porque me falta a simplicidade divina
De ser todo só o meu exterior.

Olho e comovo-me,
Comovo-me como a água corre quando o chão é inclinado,
E a minha poesia é natural como o levantar-se o vento . . .

XXVIII. Li hoje quase duas páginas

Li hoje quase duas páginas
Do livro dum poeta místico,
E ri como quem tem chorado muito.

Os poetas místicos são filósofos doentes,
E os filósofos são homens doidos.

Porque os poetas místicos dizem que as flores sentem
E dizem que as pedras têm alma
E que os rios têm êxtases ao luar.

Mas as flores, se sentissem, não eram flores,
Eram gente;
E se as pedras tivessem alma, eram coisas vivas, não eram pedras;
E se os rios tivessem êxtases ao luar,
Os rios seriam homens doentes.

E preciso não saber o que são flores e pedras e rios
Para falar dos sentimentos deles.
Falar da alma das pedras, das flores, dos rios,
É falar de si próprio e dos seus falsos pensamentos.
Graças a Deus que as pedras são só pedras,
É que os rios não são senão rios,
E que as flores são apenas flores.

XIV. Rhymes mean nothing to me

Rhymes mean nothing to me. Only rarely
Are two trees identical, standing side by side.
To me, thinking and writing come naturally, as color to a flower,
But I'm less perfect in my way of putting things
Because I lack the divine simplicity
Of being only what I appear to be.

I look and I am moved
As water is when it flows downhill.
And my poetry is natural as the rising of the wind . . .

XXVIII. Today I read nearly two pages

Today I read nearly two pages
In a book by a mystic poet
And I laughed like someone who'd been sobbing.

Mystic poets are sick philosophers,
And philosophers are mad men.

Because mystic poets say that flowers feel
And say that stones have souls
And rivers have ecstasies in moonlight.

But flowers wouldn't be flowers if they felt anything—
They'd be people;
And if stones had souls they'd be living things, not stones;
And if rivers had ecstasies in moonlight,
They'd be sick people.

Only if you don't know what flowers, stones, and rivers are
Can you talk about their feelings.
To talk about the souls of flowers, stones, and rivers
Is to talk about yourself, about your delusions.
Thank God stones are just stones,
And rivers, just rivers,
And flowers, just flowers.

Por mim, escrevo a prosa dos meus versos
E fico contente,
Porque sei que compreendo a Natureza por fora;
E não a compreendo por dentro
Porque a Natureza não tem dentro;
Senão não era a Natureza.

XXX. Se quiserem que eu tenha um misticismo

Se quiserem que eu tenha um misticismo, está bem, tenho-o.
Sou místico, mas só com o corpo.
A minha alma é simples e não pensa.

O meu misticismo é não querer saber.
É viver e não pensar nisso.

Não sei o que é a Natureza: canto-a.
Vivo no cimo dum outeiro
Numa casa caiada e sòzinha,
E essa é a minha definição.

XXXII. Ontem à tarde um homen das cidades

Ontem à tarde um homem das cidades
Falava à porta da estalagem.
Falava comigo também.

Falava da justiça e da luta para haver justiça
E dos operários que sofrem,
E do trabalho constante, e dos que têm fome,
E dos ricos, que só têm costas para isso.

E, olhando para mim, viu-me lágrimas nos olhos
E sorriu com agrado, julgando que eu sentia
O ódio que ele sentia, e a compaixão
Que ele dizia que sentia.

As for myself, I write out the prose of my poems,
And I am satisfied,
Because I know that all I know is Nature from the outside;
I don't understand it from the inside,
Because Nature hasn't any inside;
Otherwise, it wouldn't be Nature.

XXX. If they want me to be a mystic, fine. So I'm a mystic.

If they want me to be a mystic, fine. So I'm a mystic.
I'm a mystic, but only of the body.
My soul is simple; it doesn't think.

My mysticism consists in not desiring to know,
In living without thinking about it.

I don't know what Nature is; I sing it.
I live on a hilltop
In a solitary cabin.
And that's what it's all about.

XXXII. Yesterday afternoon a city man

Yesterday afternoon a city man
Was talking at the door of the inn.
He was talking to me too.

He spoke of justice and the struggle for justice,
And of the suffering workers,
Of ceaseless toil, and of hungry people,
And of the rich who just turn their backs to it all.

And, looking at me, he saw I had tears in my eyes,
And that pleased him, thinking I felt
The hatred he felt, and the compassion
He said he felt.

(Mas eu mal o estava ouvindo.
Que me importam a mim os homens
E o que sofrem ou supõem que sofrem?
Sejam como eu — não sofrerão.
Todo o mal do mundo vem de nos importarmos uns com os outros,
Quer para fazer bem, quer para fazer mal.
A nossa alma e o céu e a terra bastam-nos.
Querer mais é perder isto, e ser infeliz).

Eu no que estava pensando
Quando o amigo de gente falava
(E isso me comoveu até às lágrimas),
Era em como o murmúrio longínquo dos chocalhos
A esse entardecer
Não parecia os sinos duma capela pequenina
A que fossem à missa as flores e os regatos
E as almas simples como a minha.

(Louvado seja Deus que não sou bom,
E tenho o egoísmo natural das flores
E dos rios que seguem o seu caminho
Preocupados sem o saber
Só com o florir e ir correndo.
É essa a única missão no Mundo,
Essa — existir claramente,
E saber fazê-lo sem pensar nisso).

E o homem calara-se, olhando o poente.
Mas que tem com o poente quem odeia e ama?

XLIII. Antes o vôo da ave

Antes a vôo da ave, que passa e não deixa rasto,
Que a passagem do animal, que fica lembrada no chão.
A ave passa e esquece, e assim deve ser.
O animal, onde já não está e por isso de nada serve,
Mostra que já esteve, o que não serve para nada.

(But I was scarcely listening.
What do I care about mankind
And their suffering or what they think they're suffering?
Let them be like me, and they won't suffer.
All the world's troubles come from our worrying about one
        another—
Whether to do good or do evil.
Our own souls, the earth and the sky, are all we need.
To want more is to lose these things and be unhappy.)

What I was thinking about
While the friend of mankind was talking
(And what moved me to tears),
Was that the tinkle of distant cowbells
As night came on
Seemed nothing like the sound of bells in a small chapel
Where flowers and brooks might go to Mass
Along with simple souls like me.

(Thank God I'm not good,
And have the natural egoism of flowers
And of rivers going their way,
Kept busy, without knowing it,
Only with flowering and flowing.
That's the only mission there is in the world—
To exist clearly
And to know how, without thinking about it.)

And the man fell silent, watching the sunset.
But a man who hates and loves, what's he got to do with sunsets?

XLIII. Rather the bird flying by

Rather the bird flying by and leaving no trace
Than the passing beast leaving tracks in the earth.
The bird going by is forgotten, and should be.
The beast, no longer there (and so perfectly useless),
Shows it was there (also perfectly useless).

A recordação é uma traição à Natureza,
Porque a Natureza de ontem não é Natureza.
O que foi não é nada, e lembrar é não ver.

Passa, ave, passa, e ensina-me a passar!

XLVII. Num dia excessivamente nítido

Num dia excessivamente nítido,
Dia em que dava a vontande de ter trabalhado muito
Para nele não trabalhar nada,
Entrevi, como uma estrada por entre as árvores,
O que talvez seja o Grande Segredo,
Aquele Grande Mistério de que os poetas falsos falam.

Vi que não há Natureza,
Que Natureza não existe,
Que há montes, vales, planícies,
Que há árvores, flores, ervas,
Que há rios e pedras,
Mas que não há um todo a que isso pertença,
Que um conjunto real e verdadeiro
É uma doença das nossas ideias.

A Natureza é partes sem um todo.
Isto é talvez o tal mistério de que falam.

Foi isto o que sem pensar nem parar,
Acertei que devia ser a verdade
Que todos andam a achar e que não acham,
E que só eu, porque a não fui achar, achei.

Remembering betrays Nature
Because yesterday's Nature is not Nature.
What's past is nothing; remembering is seeing nothing.

Fly, bird, fly away; teach me to disappear!

XLVIII. On a terribly clear day

On a terribly clear day,
A day that made you wish you'd already worked very hard
So as to be free to do nothing at all,
I caught a glimpse, like a road through the trees,
Of what might after all be the Big Secret,
That Great Mystery deceitful poets talk about.

I saw that there is no Nature,
That Nature doesn't exist,
That there are hills, valleys, plains,
That there are trees, flowers, grasses,
That there are streams and stones,
But that there's no one great All these things belong to,
That any really authentic unity
Is a sickness of our thinking.

Nature is simply parts, nothing whole.
Maybe this is the mystery they talk about.

And this, without my stopping to think about it,
Is just what I hit on as being the truth
That everyone goes around looking for in vain,
And that only I, because I wasn't looking, found.

Dizes-me: tu és mais alguma coisa

Dizes-me: tu és mais alguma coisa
Que uma pedra ou uma planta.
Dizes-me: sentes, pensas e sabes
Que pensas e sentes.
Então as pedras escrevem versos?
Então as plantas têm ideias sobre o mundo?

Sim: há diferença.
Mas não é a diferença que encontras;
Porque o ter consciência não me obriga a ter teorias sobre as coisas:
Só me obriga a ser consciente.

Se sou mais que uma pedra ou uma planta? Não sei.
Sou diferente. Não sei o que é mais ou menos.

Ter consciência é mais que ter cor?
Pode ser e pode não ser.
Sei que é diferente apenas.
Ninguém pode provar que é mais que só diferente.

Sei que a pedra é a real, e que a planta existe.
Sei isto porque elas existem.
Sei isto porque os meus sentidos me mostram.
Sei que sou real também.
Sei isto porque os meus sentidos me mostram,
Embora com menos clareza que me mostram a pedra e a planta.
Não sei mais nada.

Sim, escrevo versos, e a pedra não escreve versos.
Sim, faço ideias sobre o mundo, e a planta nenhumas.
Mas é que as pedras não são poetas, são pedras;
E as plantas são plantas só, e não pensadores.

from *Disjunctive Poems*

You tell me: but you're something more

You tell me: but you're something more
Than a stone or a plant.
You tell me: you feel, you think, and now
That you feel and think.
Besides, do stones write verses?
And do plants have ideas about the world?

Yes: there's a difference.
But not the difference you think there is.
Because being aware doesn't make me have theories about things.
It only makes me aware.

Am I more than a stone or a plant? I don't know.
I'm different. I don't know what *more* is or *less*.

Is having consciousness greater than having color?
Possibly, but possibly not.
I only know that it's different.
No one can prove it's more than different.

I know the stone is real and the plant exists.
I know this because they exist.
I know this because my senses tell me so.
I also know I'm real.
I know it because my senses tell me so,
Though they tell me this less plainly than they tell me about
stones and plants.
That's all I know.

Yes, I write verses, and the stone doesn't.
Yes, I have ideas about the world, and the plant hasn't any.
But stones aren't poets; they're stones.
And plants are plants, not thinkers.

Tanto posso dizer que sou superior a elas por isto,
Como que sou inferior.
Mas não digo isso: digo da pedra, «é uma pedra»,
Digo da planta, «é uma planta»,
Digo de mim, «sou eu».
E não digo mais nada. Que mais há a dizer?

A espantosa realidade das coisas

A espantosa realidade das coisas
É a minha descoberta de todos os dias.
Cada coisa é o que é,
E é difícil explicar a alguém quanto isso me alegra,
E quanto isso me basta.

Basta existir para se ser completo.

Tenho escrito bastantes poemas.
Hei-de escrever muitos mais, naturalmente.
Cada poema meu diz isto,
E todos os meus poemas são diferentes,
Porque cada coisa que há é uma maneira de dizer isto.

Às vezes ponho-me a olhar para uma pedra.
Não me ponho a pensar se ela sente.
Não me perco a chamar-lhe minha irmã.
Mas gosto dela por ela ser uma pedra,
Gosto dela porque ela não sente nada,
Gosto dela porque ela não tem parentesco nenhum comigo.

Outras vezes oiço passar o vento,
E acho que só para ouvir passar o vento vale a pena ter nascido.

I can no more say I'm superior to them on that account
Than that I'm inferior.
But I don't claim to be superior or inferior.
Of the stone I say, it's a stone.
Of the plant I say, it's a plant.
Of myself I say, I am me.
And I can't say any more. What more is there to say?

The frightening reality of things

The frightening reality of things
Is my discovery every single day.
Every thing is what it is,
And it's hard to explain to anyone how much this delights me
And suffices me.

To be whole, it is enough simply to exist.

I've written a good many poems.
I shall write many more, naturally.
Each of my poems speaks of this,
And yet all my poems are different,
Because each thing that exists is one way of saying this.

Sometimes I start looking at a stone.
I don't start by thinking, Does it have feeling?
I don't force myself to call it my sister.
But I get pleasure out of its being a stone,
Enjoying it because it feels nothing,
Enjoying it because it's not at all related to me.

Occasionally I hear the wind blow,
And I find that just hearing the wind blow makes it
                                        worth having been born.

Eu não sei o que é que os outros pensarão lendo isto;
Mas acho que isto deve estar bem porque o penso sem esforço,
Nem ideia de outras pessoas a ouvir-me pensar;
Porque o penso sem pensamentos,
Porque o digo como as minhas palavras o dizem.

Uma vez chamaram-me poeta materialista,
E eu admirei-me, porque não julgava
Que se me pudesse chamar qualquer coisa.
Eu nem sequer sou poeta: vejo.
Se o que escrevo tem valor, não sou eu que o tenho:
O valor está ali, nos meus versos.
Tudo isso é absolutamente independente da minha vontade.

I don't know what others reading this will think;
But I find it must be good since it's what I think without effort,
With no idea that other people are listening to me think it;
Because I think it without thoughts,
Because I say it as my words say it.

I was once called a materialist poet
And was surprised, because I didn't imagine
I could be called anything at all.
I'm not even a poet: I see.
If what I write has any merit, it's not in me;
The merit is there, in my verses.
All this is absolutely independent of my will.

2
Ricardo Reis

As rosas amo dos jardins do Adónis

As rosas amo dos jardins de Adónis,
Essas volucres amo, Lídia, rosas,
    Que em o dia em que nascem,
    Em esse dia morrem.
A luz para elas é eterna, porque
Nascem nascido já o sol, e acabam
    Antes que Apolo deixe
    O seu curso visível.
Assim façamos nossa vida *um dia,*
Inscientes, Lídia, voluntàriamente
    Que há noite antes e após
    O pouco que duramos.

Já sobre a fronte vã me acinzenta

Já sobre a fronte vã se me acinzenta
O cabelo do jovem que perdi.
    Meus olhos brilham menos.
Já não tem jus a beijos minha boca.
Se me ainda amas, por amor não ames:
    Traíras-me comigo.

Tudo que cessa é morte

Tudo que cessa é morte, e a morte é nossa
Se é para nós que cessa. Aquele arbusto
    Fenece, e vai com ele
    Parte da minha vida.
Em tudo quanto olhei fiquei em parte.
Com tudo quanto vi, se passa, passo,
    Nem distingue a memória
    Do que vi do que fui.

from *Odes*

I the roses love in the gardens of Adonis

I the roses love in the gardens of Adonis,
Lydia, I love those fast fleeting roses
    That on the day they are born,
    On that same day they die.
Light for them is everlasting: born
After the sun comes up, they die
    Before Apollo rounds
    His visible track.
So let us make our life *a single day,*
And willingly ignore the night to come,
    The night already past,
    The little while we last.

Now hoary gray descends upon the brows

Now hoary gray descends upon the brows
Of the youth I was and lost.
    My eyes gleam less and less.
My lips no longer have the right to kiss.
If you should love me still, for love's own sake, desist:
    You betray me with myself.

Whatever stops is death, and is our death

Whatever stops is death, and is our death
If it stops for us. That very shrub now
    Withering, takes with it
    Part of my present life.
In everything I saw, part of me remained.
With all I saw that passed I passed on too.
    Nor does memory distinguish
    What I saw from what I was.

Se recordo quem fui, outram me vejo

Se recordo quem fui, outrem me vejo,
E o passado é o presente na lembrança.
    Quem fui é alguém que amo
    Porém sòmente em sonho.
E a saudade que me aflige a mente
Não é de mim nem do passado visto,
    Senão de quem habito
    Por tràs dos olhos cegos.
Nada, senão o instante, me conhece.
Minha mesma lembrança é nada, e sinto
    Que quem sou e quem fui
    São sonhos diferentes.

Quando, Lídia, vier o nosso Outono

Quando, Lídia, vier o nosso Outono
Com o Inverno que há nele, reservemos
Um pensamento, não para a futura
    Primavera, que é de outrem,
Nem para o Estio, de quem somos mortos,
Senão para o que fica do que passa—
O amarelo actual que as folhas vivem
    E as torna diferentes.

Ninguém, na vasta selva virgem

Ninguém, na vasta selva virgem
Do mundo inumerável, finalmente
    Vê o Deus que conhece.
Só o que a brisa traz se ouve na brisa
O que pensamos, seja amor ou deuses,
    Passa, porque passamos.

Recalling who I was, I see somebody else.

Recalling who I was, I see somebody else.
In memory the past becomes the present.
    Who I was is somebody I love,
    Yet only in a dream.
The sadness that torments me now
Is not for me nor for the past invoked,
    But for him who lives in me
    Behind blind eyes.
Nothing knows me but the moment.
Even my memory is nothing, and I feel
    That who I am and who I was
    Are two contrasting dreams.

Lydia, when our Autumn comes

Lydia, when our Autumn comes,
Bearing Winter with it, let us keep
One thought: not of Spring
To come, belonging to another,
Nor yet of Summer, in which we are dead,
But of what is left of what is passing.
It is the yellowing of these leaves now
    Makes them different.

No one, in the vast and virgin jungle

No one, in the vast and virgin jungle
Of this unreckoned world, ever sees
    The God he knows.
Only what is borne upon the wind, upon the wind is heard.
All we ponder, our loves, our gods,
    Pass on, because we do.

Lídia, ignoramos

Lídia, ignoramos. Somos estrangeiros
Onde quer que estejamos.

Lídia, ignoramos. Somos estrangeiros
Onde quer que moremos. Tudo é alheio
Nem fala língua nossa.
Façamos de nós mesmos o retiro
Onde esconder-nos, tímidos do insulto
Do tumulto do mundo.
Que quer o amor mais que não ser dos outros?
Como um segredo dito nos mistérios,
Seja sacro por nosso.

Para ser grande, sê inteiro

Para ser grande, sê inteiro: nada
     Teu exagera ou exclui.
Sê todo em cada coisa. Põe quanto és
     No mínimo que fazes.
Assim em cada lago a lua toda
     Brilha, porque alta vive.

Quero dos deuses só que me não lembrem.

Quero dos deuses só que me não lembrem.
Serei livre—sem dita nem desdita,
Como o vento que é a vida
Do ar que não é nada.
O ódio e o amor iguais nos buscam; ambos,
Cada um com seu modo, nos oprimem.
     A quem deuses concedem
     Nada, tem liberdade.

Lydia, we know nothing. We are strangers

Lydia, we know nothing. We are strangers
Whatever we may be.

Lydia, we know nothing. We are strangers
Wherever we may live. Everything is alien,
No one speaks our language.
Let us in ourselves create a refuge,
And from the hurt and tumult
Of the world withdraw.
What more can love desire than not to let the others in?
Like a secret uttered in a mystery,
Let this become our sanctuary.

To be great, be whole

To be great, be whole; exclude
    Nothing, exaggerate nothing that is you.
Be whole in everything. Put all you are
    Into the smallest thing you do.
The whole moon gleams in every pool,
    It rides so high.

Para ser grande,
hay que ser
completo

I ask the gods only to forget me.

I ask the gods only to forget me.
Neither sad nor glad, I shall be free,
Free as the wind is, giving life
To the air that is nothing.
Love and hatred seek us out, both
Oppressively, each differently.
                Only he is free
                To whom the gods grant nothing.

Aos deuses peço só

Aos deuses peço só que me concedam
O nada lhes pedir. A dita é um jugo
      E o ser feliz oprime
Porque é um certo estado.
Não quieto nem inquieto meu ser calmo
Quero erguer alto acima de onde os homens
      Têm prazer ou dores.

I only ask the gods to grant me

I only ask the gods to grant me
That I ask nothing of them. Happiness is a burden,
      Good fortune is a yoke,
Both bespeaking too secure a state.
Not composed nor discomposed, I would calmly live
Beyond that state in which men take
      To sorrows and to joys.

3

Alvaro de Campos

Tenho uma grande contipação

Tenho uma grande constipação
E toda a gente sabe como as grandes constipações
Alteram todo o sistema do universo,
Zangam-nos contra a vida,
E fazem espirrar até à metafísica.
Tenho o dia perdido cheio de me assoar.
Dói-me a cabeça indistintamente.
Triste condição para um poeta menor!
Hoje sou verdadeiramente um poeta menor.
O que fui outrora foi um desejo; partiu-se.

Adeus para sempre, rainha das fadas!
As tuas asas eram de sol, e eu cá vou andando.
Não estarei bem se não me deitar na cama.
Nunca estive bem senão deitando-me no universo.

Excusez un peu... Que grande constipação física!
Preciso de verdade e da aspirina.

O sono que desce sobre mim

O sono que desce sobre mim,
O sono mental que desce fisicamente sobre mim,
O sono universal que desce individualmente sobre mim—
Esse sono
Parecerá aos outros o sono de dormir,
O sono da vontade de dormir,
O sono de ser sono.

Mas é mais, mais de dentro, mais de cima:
É o sono da soma de todas as desilusões,

from *Poems*

I have a terrible cold

I have a terrible cold.
And everyone knows how terrible colds
Change the whole structure of the universe,
Making us sore at life,
Making us sneeze till we get metaphysical.
My day is wasted, full of blowing my nose.
My head aches vaguely.
A sad fix for a minor poet to be in!
Today I'm really a minor poet.
Whatever I was turns into a dream-wish that's disappeared.

Fairy queen, goodbye forever!
Your wings were sunbeams, and my feet are clay.
I'll never be well if I don't get to bed.
I never was well unless I was stretched out across the universe.

Excusez un peu . . . What a terrible physical cold!
I need some truth and aspirin.

The sleep that comes over me

The sleep that comes over me,
The mental sleep that physically hits me,
The universal sleep that personally overcomes me—
To others
Such a sleep must seem a sleep to fall asleep in,
The sleep of someone wanting to go to sleep,
The very sleep that is sleep.

But it's more, it goes deeper, higher than that:
It's the sleep that tops all disillusionment,

E o sono da síntese de todas as desesperanças,
É o sono de haver mundo comigo lá dentro
Sem que eu houvesse contribuído em nada para isso.

O sono que desce sobre mim
É contudo como todos os sonos.
O cansaço tem ao menos brandura,
O abatimento tem ao menos sossego,
A rendição é ao menos o fim do esforço,
O fim é ao menos o já não haver que esperar.

Há um som de abrir uma janela,
Viro indiferente a cabeça para a esquerda
Por sobre o ombro que a sente,
Olho pela janela entreaberta:
A rapariga do segundo-andar de defronte
Debruça-se com os olhos azuis à procura de alguém.
De quem?,
Pergunta a minha indiferença.
E tudo isso é sono.

Meu Deus, tanto sono! . . .

Saudação a Walt Whitman

Portugal-Infinito, onze de Junho de mil novecentos e quinze . . .
Hé-lá-á-á-á-á-á-á!

De aqui de Portugal, todas as épocas no meu cérebro,
Saúdo-te, Walt, saúdo-te, meu irmão em Universo,
Eu, de monóculo e casaco exageradamente cintado,
Não sou indigno de ti, bem o sabes, Walt,
Não sou indigno de ti, basta saudar-te para o não ser . . .
Eu tão contíguo à inércia, tão fàcilmente cheio de tédio,
Sou dos teus, tu bem sabes, e compreendo-te e amo-te,
E embora te não conhecesse, nascido pelo ano em que morrias,
Sei que me amaste também, que me conheceste, e estou contente.

It's the sleep that synthesizes all despair,
It's the sleep of feeling the world has swallowed me
Without my having said yes or no to it.

Yet the sleep that comes over me
Is just like ordinary sleep.
Being tired at least softens you up,
Being rundown at least numbs you,
Giving up at least puts an end to trying,
And the end at least is giving up hope.

There's the sound of a window opening.
Indifferent, I turn my head to the left,
Looking over the shoulder that felt it,
And see through a half-opened window
The girl on the second floor across the street
Leaning out, her blue eyes searching for someone.
Who?
My indifference asks.
And all this is sleep.

My God, so much sleep! . . .

Salutation to Walt Whitman

Infinite Portugal, June eleventh, nineteen hundred and fifteen . . .
A-hoy-hoy-hoy-hoy!

From here in Portugal, with all the ages in my brain,
I salute you, Walt, I salute you, my brother in the Universe,
I, with my monocle and tightly buttoned frock coat,
I am not unworthy of you, Walt, as you well know,
I am not unworthy of you, as my greeting you shows . . .
I, so like you in indolence, so easily bored,
I am with you, as you well know, and understand you and love you,
And though I never met you, born the same year you died,
I know you loved me too, you knew me and I am happy.

Sei que me conheceste, que me contemplaste e me explicaste,
Sei que é isso que eu sou, quer em Brooklyn Ferry dez anos antes
                                                de eu nascer,
Quer pela rua do Ouro acima pensando em tudo que não é a rua do Ouro
E conforme tu sentiste tudo, sinto tudo, e cá estamos de mãos dadas,
De mãos dadas, Walt, de mãos dadas, dançando o universo na alma.

Ó sempre moderno e eterno, cantor dos concretos absolutos,
Concubina fogosa do universo disperso,
Grande pederasta roçando-te contra diversidade das coisas,
Sexualizado pelas pedras, pelas árvores, pelas pessoas, pelas profissões,
Cio das passagens, dos encotros casuais, das meras observações,
Meu entusiasta pelo conteúdo de tudo,
Meu grande herói entrando pela Morte dentro aos pinotes,
E aos urros, e aos guinchos, e aos berros saudando Deus!

Cantor da fraternidade feroz e terna com tudo,
Grande democrata epidérmico, contíguo a tudo em corpo e alma,
Carnaval de todas as acções, bacanal de todos os propósitos,
Irmão gémeo de todos os arrancos,
Jean-Jacques Rousseau do mundo que havia de produzir máquinas,
Homero do *insaisissable* do flutuante carnal,
Shakespeare da sensação que começa a andar a vapor,
Milton-Shelley do horizonte da Electricidade futura!
Íncubo de todos os gestos,
Espasmo pra dentro de todos os objectos-força,
Souteneur de todo o Universo,
Rameira de todos os sistemas solares...

Quantas vezes eu beijo o teu retrato!
Lá onde estás agora (não sei onde é mas é Deus)
Sentes isto, sei que o sentes, e os meus beijos são mais quentes
                                                (em gente)

I know that you knew me, that you considered me and explained me,
I know that this is what I am, whether on Brooklyn Ferry ten
                              years before I was born
Or strolling up *Rua do Ouro** thinking about everything that is
                              not *Rua do Ouro,*
And just as you felt everything, so I feel everything, and so
                              here we are clasping hands,
Clasping hands, Walt, clasping hands, with the universe doing
                              a dance in our soul.

O singer of concrete absolutes, always modern and eternal,
Fiery concubine of the scattered world,
Great pederast brushing up against the diversity of things,
Sexualized by rocks, by trees, by people, by their trades,
Rutting on the move, with casual encounters, with mere
                              observations,
My enthusiast for the contents of everything,
My great hero going to meet death by leaps and bounds,
Roaring, screaming, bellowing greetings to God!

Singer of cruel and tender brotherhood with everything,
Great epidermic democrat, close to all in body and soul,
Carnival of all deeds, bacchanalia of all intentions,
Twin brother of all impulses,
Jean-Jacques Rousseau of the world destined to produce machines,
Homer of all ungraspable and wavering carnality,
Shakespeare of the sensation that begins to be steam-propelled,
Milton-Shelley of the dawn of Electricity!
Incubus of all gestures,
Inner spasm of all force in objects,
Pimp of the whole Universe,
Whore of all solar systems . . .

How many times have I kissed your picture!
Wherever you are now (I don't know where it is but it is God),
You feel this, I know you feel it, and my kisses are warmer
                              (among us)

*The main commercial and financial thoroughfare in Lisbon, equivalent in a way to
Wall Street—literally, Gold Street. (E.H.)

E tu assim é que os queres, meu velho, e agradeces de lá, —
Sei-o bem, qualquer coisa mo diz, um agrado no meu espírito

Uma erecção abstracta e indirecta no fundo da minha alma.

Nada do *engageant* em ti, mas ciclópico e musculoso,
Mas perante o Universo a tua atitude era de mulher,
E cada erva, cada pedra, cada homem era para ti o Universo.

Meu velho Walt, meu grande Camarada, evohé!
Pertenço a tua orgia báquica de sensações-em-liberdade,
Sou dos teus, desde a sensação dos meus pés até à náusea em
                                              meus sonhos,
Sou dos teus, olha pra mim, de aí desde Deus vês-me ao contrário:
De dentro para fora. . . Meu corpo é o que adivinhas, vês a minha alma—
Essa vês tu pròpriamente e através dos olhos dela o meu corpo—
Olha pra mim: tu sabes que eu, Álvaro de Campos, engenheiro,
Poeta sensacionista,
Não sou teu discípulo, não sou teu amigo, não sou teu cantor,
Tu sabes que eu sou Tu e estás contente com isso!

Nunca posso ler os teus versos a fio. . . Há ali sentir demais. . .
Atravesso os teus versos como uma multidão aos encontrões a mim,
E cheira-me a suor, a óleos, a actividade humana e mecânica.
Nos teus versos, a certa altura não sei se leio ou se vivo,
Não sei se o meu lugar real é no mundo ou nos teus versos,

Não sei se estou aqui, de pé sobre a terra natural,
Ou de cabeça pra baixo, pendurado numa espécie de estabelecimento,
No tecto natural da tua inspiração de tropel,
No centro do tecto da tua intensidade inacessível.

And you like it that way, dear old man, and you thank me
                     for them—
I know this well, something tells me, like a feeling of pleasant
                     warmth in my spirit,

An abstract, oblique erection at the bottom of my soul.

There was nothing of the *engageant* in you—rather the muscular,
                     the cyclopic,
Though in facing the Universe yours was the attitude of a woman,
For every blade of grass, every stone, every man was a Universe
                     for you.

Walt, my beloved old man, my great Comrade, I evoke you!
I belong to your Bacchic orgy of free sensations,
I am yours, from the tingling of my toes to the nausea of my
                     dreams,
I am yours, look at me—up there where you are near God,
                     you see me contrariwise,
From inside out . . . My body is what you divine but you see
                     my soul—
You see it properly, and through its eyes you glimpse my body—
Look at me: you know that I, Alvaro de Campos, engineer,
Sensationist poet,
Am not your disciple, am not your friend, am not your singer,
You know that I am You, and you are happy about it!

I could never read all your verses through . . . There's too much
                     feeling in them . . .
I go through your lines as through a teeming crowd brushing
                     past me,
And I smell the sweat, the grease, the human and mechanical
                     activity.
At a given moment, reading your poems, I can't tell if I'm reading
                     or living them,
I don't know if my actual place is in the world or in your verse,

I don't know if I'm standing here, with both feet on the ground,
Or hanging upside down in some sort of institution,
From the natural ceiling of your tumultuous inspiration,
From the middle of the ceiling of your inaccessible intensity.

Abram-me todas as portas!
Por força que hei-de passar!
Minha senha? Walt Whitman!
Mas não dou senha nenhuma . . .
Passo sem explicações . . .
Se for preciso meto dentro as portas . . .
Sim — eu, franzino e civilizado, meto dentro as portas,
Porque neste momento não sou franzino nem civilizado,
Sou EU, um universo pensante de carne e osso, querendo passar,
E que há-de passar por força, porque quando quero passar sou Deus!

Tirem esse lixo da minha frente!
Metam-me em gavetas essas emoções!
Daqui pra fora, politicos, literatos,
Comerciantes pacatos, polícia, meretrizes, *souteneurs,*
Tudo isso é a letra que mata, não o espírito que dá a vida.
O espírito que dá a vida neste momento sou EU!

Que nenhum filho da . . . se me atravesse no caminho!
O meu caminho é pelo infinito fora até chegar ao fim!
Se sou capaz de chegar ao fim ou não, não é contigo,
É comigo, com Deus, com o sentido—eu da palavra Infinito . . .
Prá frente!
Meto esporas!
Sinto as esporas, sou o próprio cavalo em que monto,
Porque eu, por minha vontade de me consubstanciar com Deus,
Posso ser tudo, ou posso ser nada, ou qualquer coisa,
Conforme me der na gana . . . Ninguém tem nada com isso . . .
Loucura furiosa! Vontade de ganir, de saltar,
De urrar, zurrar, dar pulos, pinotes, gritos com o corpo,
De me *cramponner* às rodas dos veículos e meter por baixo,
De me meter adiante do giro do chicote que vai bater,
De ser a cadela de todos os cães e eles não bastam,
De ser o volante de todas as máquinas e a velocidâde tem limite,
De ser o esmagado, o deixado, o deslocado, o acabado,
Dança comigo, Walt, lá do outro mundo, esta fúria,
Salta comigo neste batuque que esbarra com os astros,

Open all the doors for me!
Because I have to go in!
My password? Walt Whitman!
But I don't give any password . . .
I go in without explaining . . .
If I must, I'll knock the doors down . . .
Yes, slight and civilized though I am, I'll knock the doors down,
Because at this moment I'm not slight or civilized at all,
I'm ME, a thinking universe of flesh and bone, wanting to get in
And having to get in by force, because when I want to go in
                          I am God!

Take this garbage out of my way!
Put those emotions away in drawers!
Get out of here, you politicians, literati,
You peaceful businessmen, policemen, whores, pimps,
All your kind is the letter that kills, not the spirit giving life.
The spirit giving life at this moment is ME!

Let no son of a bitch get in my way!
My path goes through Infinity before reaching its end!
It's not up to you whether I reach this end or not,
It's up to me, up to God—up to what I mean by the word *Infinite* . . .
Go on!
Press onward!
I feel the spurs, I am the very horse I mount
Because I, since I want to be consubstantial with God,
Can be everything, or I can be nothing, or anything,
Just as I please . . . It's nobody's business . . .
Raging madness! Wanting to yelp, jump,
Scream, bray, do handsprings and somersaults, my body yelling,
Wanting to grab hold of car wheels and go under them,
Get inside the whirling whip that's about to strike,
Be the bitch to all dogs and they not enough for me,
Be the steering wheel of all machines and their limitless speed,
Be the one who's crushed, abandoned, dislocated, or done for,
Come dance this fury with me, Walt, you there in that other world,
Let's swing into this rock dance, knocking at the stars,

Cai comigo sem forças no chão,
Esbarra comigo tonto nas paredes,
Parte-te e esfrangalha-te comigo
Em tudo, por tudo, à roda de tudo, sem tudo,
Raiva abstracta do corpo fazendo *maelstroms* na alma. . .

Arre! Vamos lá prá frente!
Se o próprio Deus impede, vamos lá prá frente. . . Não faz diferença . .
Vamos lá prá frente sem ser para parte nenhuma . . .
Infinito! Universo! Meta sem meta! Que importa?

Deixa-me tirar a gravata e desabotoar o colarinho.
Não se pode ter muita energia com a civilização à roda do pescoço) . . .
Agora, sim, partamos, vá lá prá frente.

Numa grande *marche aux flambeaux*-todas-as-cidades-da-Europa,
Numa grande marcha guerreira a indústria, o comércio e ócio,
Numa grande corrida, numa grande subida, numa grande descida
Estrondeando, pulando, e tudo pulando comigo,
Salto a saudar-te,
Berro a saudar-te,
Desencadeio-me a saudar-te, aos pinotes, aos pinos, aos guinos!

Por isso é a ti que endereço
Meus versos saltos, meus versos pulos, meus versos espasmos
Os meus versos-ataques-histéricos,
Os meus versos que arrastam o carro dos meus nervos.

Aos trambolhões me inspiro,
Mal podendo respirar, ter-me de pé me exalto,
E os meus versos são eu não poder estoirar de viver.

Abram-me todas as janelas!
Arranquem-me todas as portas!
Puxem a casa toda para cima de mim!
Quero viver em liberdade no ar,
Quero ter gestos fora do meu corpo,
Quero correr como a chuva pelas paredes abaixo,
Quero ser pisado nas estradas largas como as pedras,
Quero ir, como as coisas pesadas, para o fundo dos mares,
Com uma voluptuosidade que já está longe de mim!

Fall exhausted to the ground with me,
Beat the walls with me like mad,
Break down, tear yourself apart with me,
Through everything, in everything, around everything, in nothing,
In an abstract body rage that stirs up maelstroms in the soul . . .

Damn it! Get going, I said!
Even if God himself stops us, let's get going . . . it makes no
                              difference . . .
Let's go on and get nowhere . . .
Infinity! Universe! End without end! What's the difference?

(Let me take off my tie, unbutton my collar.
You can't let off steam with civilization looped around your
                              neck . . .)
All right now, we're off to a flying start!

In a great torchlight parade of all the cities of Europe,
In a great military parade of industry, trade and leisure,
In a great race, a great incline, a great decline,
Thundering and leaping, and everything with me,
I jump up to salute you,
I yell out to salute you,
I burst loose to salute you, bounding, handstanding, yawping!

This is how I send you
My leaping verses, my bounding verses, my spasmodic verses,
My attacks-of-hysteria verses,
Verses that pull the cart of my nerves.

My crazy tumbling inspires me,
Barely able to breathe, I get to my feet exalted,
For the verses stem from my being unable to burst with life.

Open all the windows for me!
Throw open all doors!
Pull the whole house up over me!
I want to live freely, out in the open,
I want to make gestures outside my body,
To run like the rain streaming down over walls,
To be stepped on like stones down the broad streets,
To sink like heavy weights to the bottom of the sea,
And all this voluptuously, a feeling remote from me now!

Não quero fechos nas portas!
Não quero fechaduras nas cofres!
Quero intercalar-me, imiscuir-me, ser levado,
Quero que me façam pertença doída de qualquer outro,
Que me despejem dos caixotes,
Que me atirem aos mares,
Que me vão buscar a casa com fins obscenos,
Só para não estar sempre aqui sentado e quieto,
Só para não estar simplesmente escrevendo estes versos!

Não quero intervalos no mundo!
Quero a contiguidade penetrada e material dos objectos!
Quero que es corpos físicos sejam uns dos outros como as almas,
Não só dinâmicamente, mas estàticamente também!

Quero voar e cair de muito alto!
Ser arremessado como uma granada!
Ir parar a... Ser levado até...
Abstracto auge no fim de mim e de tudo!

Clímax a ferro e motores!
Escadaria pela velocidade acima, sem degraus!
Bomba hidráulica desancorando-me as entranhas sentidas!

Ponham-me grilhetas só para eu as partir!
Só para eu as partir com os dentes, e que os dentes sangrem
Gozo mazoquista, espasmódico a sangue, da vida!

Os marinheiros levaram-me preso,
As mãos apertaram-me no escuro,
Morri temporàriamente de senti-lo,
Seguiu-se a minh'alma a lamber o chão do cárcere privado,
E a cega-rega das impossibilidades contornando o meu acinte.

Pula, salta, toma o freio nos dentes,
Pégaso-ferro-em-brasa das minhas ânsias inquietas,
Paradeiro indeciso do meu destino a motores!

He's called Walt:

I don't want the doors bolted!
I don't want the safes locked!
I want to horn in there, put my nose in, be dragged off,
I want to be somebody else's wounded member,
I want to be spilled from crates,
I want to be thrown in the ocean,
I want them to come looking for me at home with lewd intentions—
Just so I'm not always sitting here quietly,
Just so I'm not simply writing these verses!

I'm against spaces-between in the world!
I'm for the compenetrated, material contiguity of objects!
I'm for physical bodies commingling like souls,
Not just dynamically but statically too!

I want to fly and fall from way up high!
To be thrown like a hand grenade!
To be brought to a sudden stop . . . To be lifted to . . .
The highest, abstract point of me and it all!

Climax of iron and motors!
Accelerated escalator without any stairs!
Hydraulic pump tearing out my smashed up guts!

Put me in chains, just so I can break them,
Just so I can break them with my teeth bleeding,
Bleeding away in spurts, with the masochistic joy of life!

The sailors took me prisoner,
Their hands gripped me in the dark,
For the moment I died of the pain,
My soul went on licking the floors of my private cell
While the whirling of impossibilities circled my spite.

Jump, leap, take the bit between your teeth,
Red-hot iron Pegasus of my twitching anxieties,
Wavering parking place of my motorized destiny!

He's called Walt:

Porta pra tudo!
Ponte pra tudo!
Estrada pra tudo!
Tua alma omnívora,
Tua alma ave, peixe, fera, homem, mulher.
Tua alma os dois onde estão dois,
Tua alma o um que são dois quando dois são um,
Tua alma seta, raio, espaço,
Amplexo, nexo, sexo, Texas, Carolina, New-York,
Brooklyn Ferry à tarde,
Brooklyn Ferry das idas e dos regressos,
Libertad! Democracy! Século vinte ao longe!
Pum! pum! pum! pum! pum!
PUM!

Tu, o que eras, tu o que vias, tu o que ouvias,
O sujeito e o objecto, o activo e o passivo,
Aqui e ali, em toda a parte tu,
Círculo fechando todas as possibilidades de sentir,
Marco miliário de todas as coisas que podem ser,
Deus Termo de todos os objectos que se imaginem e és tu!
Tu Hora,
Tu Minuto,
Tu Segundo!
Tu intercalado, liberto, desfraldado, ido,
Intercalamento, libertação, ida, desfraldamento,
Tu intercalador, libertador, desfraldador, remetente,
Carimbo em todas as cartas,
Nome em todos os endereços,
Mercadoria entregue, devolvida, seguindo . . .
Comboio de sensações a alma-quilómetro à hora,
À hora, ao minuto, ao segundo, PUM!

Agora que estou quase na morte e vejo tudo já claro,
Grande Libertador, volto submisso a ti.

Sem dúvida teve um fim a minha personalidade.
Sem dúvida porque se exprimiu, quis dizer qualquer coisa

Entryway to everything!
Bridge to everything!
Highway to everything!
Your omnivorous soul,
Your soul that's bird, fish, beast, man, woman,
Your soul that's two where two exist,
Your soul that's one becoming two when two are one,
Your soul that's arrow, lightning, space,
Amplex, nexus, sex and Texas, Carolina and New York,
Brooklyn Ferry in the twilight,
Brooklyn Ferry going back and forth,
Libertad! Democracy! the Twentieth Century about to dawn!
Boom! Boom! Boom! Boom! Boom!
BOOM!

You who lived it, you who saw it, you who heard it,
Subject and object, active and passive,
Here, there, everywhere you,
Circle closing off all possibilities of feeling,
Quintessence of all things that might still happen,
God-Terminus of all imaginable objects, and it is you!
You are the Hour,
You the Minute,
You the Second!
You interpolated, liberated, unfurled, and sent,
Interpolating, liberating, unfurling, sending,
You, the interpolator, liberator, unfurler, sender,
The seal on all letters,
The name on all addressed envelopes,
Goods delivered, returned, and to follow . . .
Trainful of feelings at so many soul-miles per hour,
Per hour, per minute, per second, BOOM!

Now that I'm almost dead and see everything so clearly,
I bow to you, Great Liberator.

Surely my personality has had some purpose.
Surely it meant something, since it expressed itself,

Mas hoje, olhando para trás, só uma ânsia me fica —
Não ter tido a tua calma superior a ti-próprio,
A tua libertação constelada de Noite Infinita.

Não tive talvez missão alguma na terra.

Heia que eu vou chamar
Ao privilégio ruidoso e ensurdecedor de saudar-te
Todo o formilhamento humano do Universo,
Todos os modos de todas as emoções
Todos os feitios de todos os pensamentos,
Todas as rodas, todos os volantes, todos os êmbolos da alma.

Heia que eu grito
E num cortejo de Mim até ti estardalhaçam
Com uma algaravia metafísica e real,
Com um chinfrim de coisas passado por dentro sem nexo.

Ave, salve, viva, ó grande bastardo de Apolo,
Amante impotente e fogoso das nove musas e das graças,
Funicular do Olimpio até nós e de nós ao Olimpo.

Apontamento

A minha alma partiu-se como um vaso vazio.
Caiu pela escada excessivamente abaixo.
Caiu das mãos da criada descuidada.
Caiu, fez-se em mais pedaços do que havia loiça no vaso.

Asneira? Impossível? Sei lá!
Tenho mais sensações do que tinha quando me sentia eu.
Sou um espalhamento de cacos sobre um capacho por sacudir.

Fiz barulho na queda como um vaso que se partia.
Os deuses que há debruçam-se do parapeito da escada.
E fitam os cacos que a criada deles fez de mim.

Yet looking back today, only one thing troubles me—
Not to have had your self-transcending calm,
Your star-clustered liberation from Infinite Night.

Maybe I had no mission at all on earth.

That's why I'm calling out,
For the ear-splitting privilege of greeting you,
All the ant-swarming humanity in the Universe,
All the ways of expressing all emotions,
All the consequences of all thoughts,
All the wheels, all the gears, all the pistons of the soul.

That's why I'm crying out
And why, in this homage to you from Me, they all begin to buzz
In their real and metaphysical gibberish,
In the uproar of things going on inside without nexus

Goodbye, bless you, live forever, O Great Bastard of Apollo,
Impotent and ardent lover of the nine muses and of the graces,
Cable-car from Olympus to us and from us to Olympus.

Note

My soul came apart like an empty jar.
It fell overwhelmingly, all the way down the stairs.
Dropped from the hands of a careless maid.
It fell. Smashed into more pieces than there was china in the jar.

Nonsense? Impossible? How should I know!
I've more sensations now than when I felt I was all me.
I'm a litter of shards strewn on a doormat about to be swept.

My fall raised a din like the crash of a jar.
The gods that exist lean over the bannister,
Staring down at the shards their maid left of me.

Não se zanguem com ela.
São tolerantes com ela.
O que eu era um vaso vazio?

Olham os cacos absurdamente conscientes,
Mas conscientes de si-mesmos, não conscientes deles.

Olham e sorriem.
Sorriem tolerantes à criada involuntária.

Alastra a grande escadaria atapetada de estrelas.
Um caco brillha, virado do exterior lustroso, entre os astros.
A minha obra? A minha alma principal? A minha vida?
Um Caco.
E os deuses olham-o especialmente, pois não sabem porque ficou ali.

Psiquetipia (Ou Psicotipia)

Símbolos. Tudo símbolos...
Se calhar, tudo é símbolos...
Serás tu um símbolo também?

Olho, desterrado de ti, as tuas mãos brancas
Postas, com boas maneiras inglesas, sobre a toalha da mesa,
Pessoas independentes de ti...
Olho-as: também serão símbolos?
Então todo o mundo é símbolo e magia?
Se calhar é...
E porque não há-de ser?

Símbolos...
Estou cansado de pensar...
Ergo finalmente os olhos para os teus olhos que me olham.
Sorris, sabendo bem em que eu estava pensando...

Meu Deus! e não sabes...
Eu pensava nos símbolos...

They aren't mad at her.
They indulge her.
After all, what was I—an empty vase?

They stare at the shards, absurdly aware,
But aware of themselves, not of the shards.

They stare down and smile.
Indulgent, they smile at the careless maid.

The big star-carpeted staircase spreads out.
A shard lies shining, polished side up, among the stars.
Is it my work? My one and only soul? My life?
A shard.
And the gods squint at it, not knowing why it still lies there.

Psychotype

Symbols. Everything's symbols . . .
It's all symbols, no doubt . . .
Can you be a symbol too?

I watch, exiled from you, your two white hands
With their good English manners propped on the tablecloth.
People independent of you . . .
I look at them: can they be symbols too?
Then the whole world is all symbol and magic?
It probably is . . .
And why shouldn't it be?

Symbols . . .
I'm tired of thinking . . .
Finally I lift my eyes to find your eyes eyeing me.
You smile, knowing just what I'm thinking . . .

My God! but you don't know . . .
I was thinking about symbols . . .

Respondo fielmente à tua conversa por cima da mesa...
«It was very strange, wasn't it?»
«Awfully strange. And how did it end?»
«Well, it didn't end. It never does, you know.»
Sim, *you know*... Eu sei...
Sim, eu sei...
É o mal dos símbolos, *you know.*
Yes, I know.
Conversa perfeitamente natural... Mas os símbolos?
Não tiro os olhos de tuas mãos... Quem são elas?
Meu Deus! Os símbolos... Os símbolos...

Poema em Linha Recta

Nunca conheci quem tivesse levado porrada.
Todos os meus conhecidos têm sido campeões em tudo.

E eu, tantas vezes reles, tantas vezes porco, tantas vezes vil,
Eu tantas vezes irrespondìvelmente parasita,
Indesculpàvelmente sujo,
Eu, que tantas vezes não tenho tido paciência para tomar banho,
Eu, que tantas vezes tenho sido ridículo, absurdo,
Que tenho enrolado os pés pùblicamente nos tapetes das etiquetas,
Que tenho sido grotesco, mesquinho, submisso e arrogante,
Que tenho sofrido enxovalhos e calado,
Que quando não tenho calado, tenho sido mais ridículo ainda;
Eu, que tenho sido cómico às criadas de hotel,
Eu, que tenho sentido o piscar de olhos dos moços de fretes,
Eu, que tenho feito vergonhas financeiras, pedido emprestado sem paga
Eu, que, quando a hora do soco surgiu, me tenho agachado.
Para fora da possibilidade do soco;
Eu, que tenho sofrido a angústia das pequenas coisas ridículas,
Eu verifico que não tenho par nisto tudo neste mundo.
Toda a gente que eu conheço e que fala comigo
Nunca teve um acto ridículo, nunca sofreu enxovalho,

Faithfully I join the conversation at the head of the table . . .
"It was very strange, wasn't it?"
"Awfully strange. And how did it end?"
"Well, it didn't end. It never does, you know."
Yes, *you know* . . . I know . . .
Yes, I know . . .
That's the trouble with symbols, *you know.*
Yes, I know.
Perfectly natural conversation . . . But symbols?
I can't take my eyes off your hands . . . Who are they?
By God! The symbols . . . The symbols . . .

Poem in a Straight Line

I don't know a soul who ever took a licking.
All my friends were champions at everything.

And I, so often vulgar, so often asinine, so often vile,
I, so deliberately parasitical,
Unforgivably filthy,
I, so often without patience to take a bath,
I, who've been so ridiculous, so absurd,
Tripping up in public on the carpet of etiquette,
I, so grotesque and mean, submissive and insolent,
Who've been insulted and not said a word,
And in not saying a word became still more ridiculous,
I who strike chambermaids as laughable,
I who feel porters wink sarcastically,
I who've been scandalous about money, borrowing and not
                              paying it back,
I, who when the time came to fight, ducked
As far as I could out of punching range,
I who go into a sweat over the slightest thing—
I'm convinced no one's better than I at this sort of game.

No one I know, none of my speaking acquaintances,
Ever acted ridiculous, ever took insults,

Nunca foi senão príncipe — todos eles príncipes — na vida...

Quem me dera ouvir de alguém a voz humana
Que confessasse não um pecado, mas uma infâmia;
Que contasse, não uma violência, mas uma cobardia!
Não, são todos o Ideal, se os oiço e me falam.
Quem há neste largo mundo que me confesse que uma vez foi vil?
Ó príncipes, meus irmãos,

Arre, estou farto de semideuses!
Onde é que há gente no mundo?

Então sou só eu que é vil e erróno nesta terra?

Poderão as mulheres não os terem amado,
Podem ter sido traídos — mas ridículos nunca!
E eu, que tenho sido ridículo sem ter sido traído,
Como posso eu falar com os meus superiores sem titubear?
Eu, que tenho sido vil, literalmente vil,
Vil no sentido mesquinho e infame da vileza.

Tabacaria

Não sou nada.
Nunca serei nada.
Não posso querer ser nada.
A parte isso, tenho em mim todos os sonhos do mundo.

Janelas do meu quarto,
Do meu quarto de um dos milhões do mundo que ninguém sabe quem é
(E se soubessem quem é, o que saberiam?),
Dais para o mistério de uma rua cruzada constantemente por gente,

Was ever anything but noble—yes, all of them princes,
                    living their lives . . .

How I'd love to hear a human voice, from any one of them,
Confessing—not to sins but to infamies,
Speaking not of violent but of cowardly acts!
But no, each one's a Paragon, or so they tell me.
Isn't there anyone in this whole world who'll confess to me
                    he's been vile just once?
All you princes, my brothers,

Enough—I'm fed up with demi-gods!
Where are the real people in this world?

Am I the only scoundrel and bungler alive?

Maybe women don't always fall for them.
Maybe they've been betrayed. But ridiculous? Never!
And I, who've been ridiculous but never betrayed,
How do I speak to their Highnesses without stammering?
I, who've been vile, so utterly vile,
Vile in the meanest and rottenest possible way.

Tobacco Shop

I'm nothing.
I'll always be nothing.
Not that I want to be nothing . . .
But aside from that, I contain all the dreams of the world
                    within me.

Windows of my room,
O room of mine—one of the world's millions nobody knows
(And if they knew it, what would they know?)—
You open on the mystery of a street that people are constantly
                    crossing,

Para uma rua inacessível a todos os pensamentos,
Real, impossìvelmente real, certa, desconhecidamente certa,
Com o mistério das coisas por baixo das pedras e dos seres,
Com a morte a pôr humidade nas paredes e cabelos brancos nos homens,
Com o Destino a conduzir a carroça de tudo pela estrada de nada.

Estou hoje vencido, como se soubesse a verdade.
Estou hoje lúcido, como se estivesse para morrer,
E não tivesse mais irmandade com as coisas
Senão uma despedida, tornando-se esta casa e este lado da rua
A fileira de carruagens de um comboio, e uma partida apitada
De dentro da minha cabeça,
E uma sacudidela dos meus nervos e um ranger de ossos na ida.

Estou hoje perplexo, como quem pensou e achou e esqueceu.
Estou hoje dividido entre a lealdade que devo
À Tabacaria do outro lado da rua, como coisa real por fora,
E à sensação de que tudo é sonho, como coisa real por dentro.

Falhei em tudo.
Como não fiz propósito nenhum, talvez tudo fosse nada.
A aprendizagem que me deram,
Desci dela pela janela das traseiras da casa.
Fui até ao campo com grandes propósitos.
Mas lá encontrei só ervas e árvores,
E quando havia gente era igual à outra.
Saio da janela, sento-me numa cadeira. Em que hei-de pensar?

Que sei eu do que serei, eu que não sei o que sou?
Ser o que penso? Mas penso ser tanta coisa!
E há tantos que pensam ser a mesma coisa que não pode haver tantos!

Génio? Neste momento
Cem mil cérebros se concebem em sonho génios como eu,

A street blocked off to all thought,
A street that's real—so impossibly real, and right—so
                              thoughtlessly right,
With the mystery of things lying under people and stones,
With death spreading dankness on walls and white hair on heads,
With fate driving each and every thing down oblivion street.

Today I'm bowled over, as if the truth had seized me.
Today I'm clearheaded, as if I were going to die,
Having barely enough brotherly feeling for things
To say goodbye, as this house and this whole side of the street
Become a line of coaches in a long long train with a whistle
                              shrieking goodbye
From inside my head,
Giving a nerve-wracking, bone-creaking jerk as it takes off.

Today I'm mixed up, like someone who thought something, grasped
                              it, then lost it.
Today I'm torn between the allegiance I owe
The Tobacco Shop across the street—something real outside me,
And the feeling that everything's a dream—something real
                              inside me.

I failed in everything.
Since I wasn't up to anything, maybe it was all really nothing.
I escaped learning anything useful
By slipping out the back window.
I went off to the country with great plans,
But found there were only trees and plants there,
And when there were people, they were just like people anywhere.
I leave my window, sit down in a chair. What should I think about?

How can I tell what I'll be—I, who don't even know what I am?
Be what I think? But I keep thinking of being so many things!
And so many people are thinking of being the same—it's
                              impossible there are so many!

Genius? At this moment
A hundred thousand heads are busy thinking they're geniuses,
                              like me,

E a história não marcará, quem sabe?, nem um,
Nem haverá senão estrume de tantas conquistas futuras.
Não, não creio em mim.
Em todos os manicómios há doidos malucos com tantas certezas!
Eu, que não tenho nenhuma certeza, sou mais certo ou menos certo?
Não, nem em mim. . .
Em quantas mansardas e não-mansardas do mundo
Não estão nesta hora génios-para-si-mesmos sonhando?
Quantas aspirações altas e nobres e lúcidas —
Sim, verdadeiramente altas e nobres e lúcidas —,
E quem sabe se realizáveis,
Nunca verão a luz do sol real nem acharão ouvidos de gente?
O mundo é para quem nasce para o conquistar
E não para quem sonha que pode conquistá-lo, ainda que tenha razão.
Tenho sonhado mais que o que Napoleão fez.
Tenho apertado ao peito hipotético mais humanidades do que Cristo,
Tenho feito filosofias em segredo que nenhum Kant escreveu.
Mas sou, e talvez serei sempre, o da mansarda,
Ainda que não more nela;
Serei sempre *o que não nasceu para isso;*
Serei sempre só *o que tinha qualidades;*
Serei sempre o que esperou que lhe abrissem a porta ao pé de
                                        uma parede sem porta
E cantou a cantiga do Infinito numa capoeira,
E ouviu a voz de Deus num poço tapado.
Crer em mim? Não, nem em nada.
Derrame-me a Natureza sobre a cabeça ardente
O seu sol, a sua chuva, o vento que me acha o cabelo,
E o resto que venha se vier, ou tiver que vir, ou não venha,
Escravos cardíacos das estrelas,
Conquistámos todo o mundo antes de nos levantar da cama;
Mas acordámos e ele é opaco,
Levantámo-nos e ele é alheio,
Saímos de casa e ele é terra inteira,
Mais o sistema solar e a Via Láctea e o Indefinido.

And who knows if history will remember even one of them.
So from all those dreams of glory there'll be nothing but
                                        manure in the end.
No, I don't believe in myself.
In every asylum there are madmen sure of almost everything!
I, certain about nothing—am I more or less sure than they?
No, not even of myself...
In how many garrets and nongarrets of the world
Are there self-styled geniuses dreaming now?
How many aspirations, noble, high, and lucid
(Yes, really noble, high, and lucid,
And, who knows, even practicable),
Will ever see the real light of day or get a hearing?
The world is made for those born to conquer it,
Nor for those who dream of conquering it, however right they
                                        may be.
I've dreamt more dreams than Napoleon ever did.
I've taken to my so-called heart more humanity than Christ did.
I've secretly thought up more philosophies than Kant ever wrote
                                        down.
Yet I am, and perhaps will always be, the man in the garret,
Even though I don't live in one;
I'll always be *the one who wasn't born for it;*
I'll always simply be *the one who had some promise;*
I'll always be the man who stood waiting for the door to open
                                        at the wall that had no door,
Who sang his anthem to Infinity in a chicken coop,
Who heard the voice of God in a sealed-up well.
Believe in myself? No, I don't, nor in anything.
Let Nature pour down on my burning head
Her sun and rain, the wind that ruffles my hair,
And all the rest—let it come, if it must, or not at all,
Cardiac cases enslaved by the stars,
We've conquered the world before getting out of bed,
But we wake and the world is opaque,
We get up and the world is strange,
We go out in the street and there's the whole earth,
Plus Solar System, Milky Way—and the Big Soup.

82

(Come chocolates, pequena;
Come chocolates!
Olha que não há mais metafísica no mundo senão chocolates.
Olha que as religiões todas não ensinam mais que a confeitaria.
Come, pequena suja, come!
Pudesse eu comer chocolates com a mesma verdade com que comes!
Mas eu penso e, ao tirar o papel de prata, que é de folhas de estanho,
Deito tudo para o chão, como tenho deitado a vida.)

Mas ao menos fica da amargura do que nunca serei
A caligrafia rápida destes versos,
Pórtico partido para o Impossível.
Mas ao menos consagro a mim mesmo um desprezo sem lágrimas,
Nobre ao menos no gesto largo com que atiro
A roupa suja que sou, sem rol, pra o decurso das coisas,
E fico em casa sem camisa.

(Tú, que consolas, que não existes e por isso consolas,
Ou deusa grega, concebida como estátua que fosse viva,
Ou patrícia romana, impossìvelmente nobre e nefasta,
Ou princesa de trovadores, gentilíssima e colorida,
Ou marquesa do século dezoito, decotada e longínqua,
Ou cocote célebre do tempo dos nossos pais,
Ou não sei quê moderno — não concebo bem o quê —,
Tudo isso, seja o que for, que sejas, se pode inspirar que inspire!
Meu coração é um balde despejado.
Como os que invocam espíritos invocam espíritos invoco
A mim mesmo e não encontro nada.
Chego à janela e vejo a rua com uma nitidez absoluta.
Vejo as lojas, vejo os passeios, vejo os carros que passam,
Vejo os entes vivos vestidos que se cruzam,
Vejo os cães que também existem,
E tudo isto me pesa como uma condenação ao degredo,
E tudo isto é estrangeiro, como tudo.)

Vivi, estudei, amei, e até cri,
E hoje não há mendigo que eu não inveje só por não ser eu.

(Go eat your chocolates, little one!
Eat your chocolates!
Look, there's no metaphysics on earth like chocolates.
Look, all the world's religions are just as edifying as making candy.
So eat, my dirty little one, eat them up!
If I could only down those chocolates as honestly as you do!
But no, I'm the thoughtful kind who peels off the silver wrapper,
                   thinks, This is only tinfoil,
And throws it all on the floor, just as I've thrown my life away.)

But at least, our of my bitterness at what I'll never be,
There's the quick calligraphy of these lines,
The broken archway to Impossibility.
And at least I reserve for myself this dry-eyed contempt—
Noble, at least, in the grand gesture I make
Of casting out the dirty clothes I am, with no laundry list, into
                   the drift of things,
And stay at home, shirtless.

(You who console me, who don't exist and therefore console me,
Whether Greek goddess, conceived as a statue that springs alive,
Or Roman matron, impossibly noble and nefarious,
Or Princess to troubadours, gentle and blushing,
Or eighteenth-century marchioness, so cool and *decolletée,*
Or famous courtesan back in our fathers' day,
Or modern whatever-you-are (since I can't say just what),
All that, whatever it is, if it can inspire, let it!
My heart's an empty pail.
Like someone who can call up spooks just calls up spooks,
I call myself up, and there's no answer.
I go back to the window and see the street in perfect clarity.
I see the shops, I see the pavement, I see the passing cars,
I see the dressed-up living passersby,
I see dogs too, also alive,
And all this weighs on me like a verdict of exile,
And all this is strange to me, like everything else.)

I lived, I studied, I loved, I even believed,
And now there's no beggar I don't envy simply for not being me.

Olho a cada um os andrajos e as chagas e a mentira,
E penso: talvez nunca vivesses nem estudasses nem amasses nem cresses
(Porque é possível fazer a realidade de tudo isso sem fazer nada disso);
Talvez tenhas existido apenas, como um lagarto a quem cortam o rabo
E que é rabo para aquém do lagarto remexidamente.

Fiz de mim o que não soube,
E o que podia fazer de mim não o fiz.
O dominó que vesti era errado.
Conheceram-me logo por quem não era e não desmenti, e perdi-me.
Quando quis tirar a máscara.
Estava pegada à cara.
Quando a tirei e me vi ao espelho,
Já tinha envelhecido.
Estava bêbado, já não sabia vestir o dominó que não tinha tirado.
Deitei fora a máscara e dormi no vestiário
Como um cão tolerado pela gerência
Por ser inofensivo
E vou escrever esta história para provar que sou sublime.

Essência musical dos meus versos inúteis,
Quem me dera encontrar-te como coisa que eu fizesse,
E não ficasse sempre defronte da Tabacaria de defronte,
Calcando aos pés a consciência de estar existindo,
Como um tapete em que um bêbado tropeça
Ou um capacho que os ciganos roubaram e não valia nada.

Mas o Dono da Tabacaria chegou à porta e ficou à porta.
Olho-o com o desconforto da cabeça mal voltada
E com o desconforto da alma mal-entendendo.
Ele morrerá e eu morrerei.
Ele deixará a tabuleta, e eu deixarei versos.
A certa altura morrerá a tabuleta também, e os versos também.
Depois de certa altura morrerá a rua onde esteve a tabuleta.

In every one I see the rags, the sores, the lies,
And think: maybe you never lived, studied, loved, believed
(Because it's possible to go through the motions without doing
                          any of it);
Maybe you barely existed, like the lizard whose tail's been snipped
And is just a tail, this side of the lizard, beating frantically.

What I made of myself, I shouldn't have,
And what I could have made of myself, I didn't.
The fancy dress I wore was the wrong one.
They saw me for what I wasn't; I didn't disabuse them,
                          so I was lost.
When I decided to take off the mask,
It stuck to my face.
When I finally took it off and looked in a mirror,
I'd grown older.
I'd been drinking, and couldn't get back into the fancy dress
                          I hadn't thrown away.
So I threw away the mask and slept in the cloakroom,
Like a dog that's let inside the house
Because it's harmless,
And I'm about to write this story to prove I'm sublime.

Musical essence of my useless lines,
If only I saw something in you that I'd made
And not something always fixed by the Tobocco Shop across
                          the street,
Kicking at the consciousness of being alive,
Like a rug some drunkard stumbles over
Or a doormat the gypsies steal that isn't worth a dime.

But the Tobacco Show Owner has come to the door and stands
                          there.
I look at him, straining my half-turned neck,
Straining my half-blind soul.
He'll die and so will I.
He'll leave his signboard, I'll leave poems.
Then after a while his signboard will perish, and so will my poems.
A little later the street will die where his signboard hung,

E a língua em que foram escritos os versos.
Morrerá depois o planeta girante em que tudo isto se deu.
Em outros satélites de outros sistemas qualquer coisa como gente
Continuará fazendo coisas como versos e vivendo por baixo de
coisas como tabuletas.
Sempre uma coisa defronte da outra,
Sempre uma coisa tão inútil como a outra,
Sempre o impossível táo estúpido como o real,
Sempre o mistério do fundo tão certo como o sono de mistério
do superfície,
Sempre isto ou sempre outra coisa ou nem uma coisa nem outra.

Mas um homem entrou na Tabacaria (para comprar tabaco?),
E a realidade plausível cai de repente em cima de mim.
Semiergo-me enérgico, convencido, humano,
E vou tencionar escrever estes versos em que digo o contrário.

Acendo um cigarro ao pensar em escrevê-los
E saboreio no cigarro a libertação de todos os pensamentos.
Sigo o fumo como rota própria,
E gozo, num momento sensitivo e competente,
A libertação de todas as especulações
E a consciência de que a metafísica é uma consequência de estar
mal disposto.

Depois deito-me para trás na cadeira
E continuo fumando.
Enquanto o Destino mo conceder, continuarei fumando.

(Se eu casasse com a filha da minha lavadeira
Talvez fosse feliz.)
Visto isto, levanto-me da cadeira. Vou à janela.

O homem saiu da Tabacaria (metendo troco na algibeira das calças?).
Ah, conheço-o: é o Esteves sem metafísica.
(O Dono da Tabacaria chegau à porta.)
Como por um instinto divino o Esteves voltou-se e viu-me.
Acenou-me adeus, gritei-lhe *Adeus ó Esteves!*, e o universo
Reconstruiu-se-me sem ideal nem esperança, e o Dono da
Tabacaria sorriu.

And so will the language my poems were written in.
Then the spinning planet will die where all this happened.
In other satellites in other systems something like people
Will go on making things like poems and living under things like
                    signboards,
always one thing standing against another,
always one thing as useless as another,
always the impossible thing as stupid as the real thing,
always the fundamental mystery as certain as the sleeping surface
                    mystery,
always this thing or that, or neither one nor the other.

But a man has gone into the Tobacco Shop (to buy tobacco?)
And the plausible reality of it all suddenly hits me.
I'm ready to get up, full of energy, convinced, human,
And about to try to write these lines, which say the opposite.

I light a cigarette and think of writing them,
And in the cigarette I taste my liberation from all thoughts.
I follow the drifting smoke like a personal highway,
For one wakeful and knowledgeable moment enjoying
The freedom from all speculation
And the consciousness that metaphysics comes out of feeling sick.

Then I fall back in my chair
And go on smoking.
As long as fate permits I'll go on smoking.

(If I married my washwoman's daughter,
Maybe I'd be happy.)
I think of this, get up from my chair. I go to the window.

The man is leaving the Shop (putting change into his pants'
                    pocket?)
Ah, I know him: it's nonmetaphysical Stevens.
(The Tobacco Shop Owner comes back to the door.)
As if by divine instinct, Stevens turns his head my way and sees me.
He waves hello, I cry *Hello Stevens!* and the universe
Reorganizes itself for me, without hopes, without ideals,
                    and the Tobacco Shop Owner smiles.

Ode Marítima

Sòzinho, no cais deserto, a esta manhã de Verão,
Olho pró lado da barra, olho pró Indefinido,
Olho e contenta-me ver,
Pequeno, negro e claro, um paquete entrando.
Vem muito longe, nítido, clássico à sua maneira.
Deixa no ar distante atrás de si a orla vã do seu fumo.
Vem entrando, e a manhã entra com ele, e no rio,
Aqui, acolá, acorda a vida marítima.
Erguem-se velas, avançam rebocadores,
Surgem barcos pequenos de trás dos navios que estão no porto.
Há uma vaga brisa.
Mas a minh'alma está com o que vejo menos,
Com o paquete que entra,
Porque ele está com a Distância, com a Manhã,
Com o sentido marítimo desta Hora,
Com a doçura dolorosa que sobe em mim como uma náusea,
Como um começar a enjoar, mas no espírito.

Olho de longe o paquete, com uma grande independência de alma,
E dentro de mim um volante começa a girar, lentamente.

Os paquetes que entram de manhã na barra
Trazem aos meus olhos consigo
O mistério alegre e triste de quem chega e parte.
Trazem memórias de cais afastados e doutros momentos
Doutro modo da mesma humanidade noutros pontos.
Todo o atracar, todo o largar de navio,
É — sinto-o em mim como o meu sangue —
Inconscientemente simbólico, terrìvelmente
Ameaçador de significações metafísicas
Que perturbam em mim quem eu fui...

Ah, todo o cais é uma saudade de pedra!
E quando o navio larga do cais
E se repara de repente que se abriu um espaço
Entre o cais e o navio,
Vem-me, não sei porquê, uma angústia recente,

Maritime Ode

Alone, on the deserted dock, this Summer morning,
I look out along the sandbar, I look out toward the Indefinite,
I look, and I am happy to see,
Small, black, and clear, a steamer approaching.
It appears so neat and classical by itself, so far away.
It leaves on the air, far behind, an empty banner of smoke.
It comes in, and the morning comes with it, and on the river
Here and there, in keeping with maritime life,
Sails are hoisted, tugboats advance,
Small boats hover behind vessels tied up at the dock.
A vague breeze rises.
But my soul belongs least with what I see,
With the approaching steamer,
Because it belongs with Distance, and with the Morning,
With the seagoing sense of this Moment,
With the sad sweetness rising in me like nausea,
Like the beginning of wanting to vomit, but spiritually . . .

I look at the far-off steamer with a great independence of spirit
And in me a flywheel begins to whir, lightly.

The steamers coming in along the sandbar in the morning
Bring with them, in my view,
The sad and happy mystery of arrivals and departures,
Bring memories of far-off docks and other moments,
Of other customs of common humanity in other places.
All the hauling in and all the sailing off of ships,
And—this I feel stirring in me as if it were my own blood—
Unconsciously symbolic, terribly portentous
With metaphysical implications
That painfully dredge up in me the man I once was . . .

Ah, the whole dock is a nostalgia of stone!
And when the ship by the dock starts to put out to sea
And then suddenly stops so that a space opens up
Between the dock and the ship,
A new dread—I don't know why—comes over me

Uma névoa de sentimentos de tristeza
Que brilha ao sol das minhas angústias relvadas
Como a primeira janela onde a madrugada bate,
E me envolve como uma recordação duma outra pessoa
Que fosse misteriosamente minha.

Ah, quem sabe, quem sabe,
Se não parti outrora, antes de mim,
Dum cais; se não deixei, navio ao sol
Oblíquo da madrugada,
Uma outra espécie de porto?
Quem sabe se não deixei, antes de a hora
Do mundo exterior como eu o vejo
Raiar-se para mim,
Um grande cais cheio de pouca gente,
Duma grande cidade meio-desperta,
Duma enorme cidade comercial, crescida, apopléctica,
Tanto quanto isso pode ser fora do Espaço e do Tempo?

Sim, dum cais, dum cais dalgum modo material,
Real, visível como cais, cais realmente,
O Cais Absoluto por cujo modelo inconscientemente imitado,
Insensìvelmente evocado,
Nós os homens construímos
Os nossos cais nos nossos portos,
Os nossos cais de pedra actual sobre água verdadeira,
Que depois de construídos se anunciam de repente
Coisas-Reais, Espíritos-Coisas, Entidades em Pedra-Almas,
A certos momentos nossos de sentimento-raiz
Quando no mundo-exterior como que se abre uma porta
E, sem que nada se altere,
Tudo se revela diverso.

Ah o Grande Cais donde partimos em Navios-Nações!
O Grande Cais Anterior, eterno e divino!
De que porto? Em que águas? E porque penso eu isto?
Grandes Cais como os outros cais, mas a Único.
Cheio como eles de silêncios rumorosos nas antemanhãs,
E desabrochando com as manhãs num ruído de guindastes
E chegadas de comboios de mercadorias,

With its mist of depressing thoughts
Glowing in the sunlight of my cropped anxieties
Like the first windowpane hit by the rising dawn,
And I am swaddled, as with the memory of some other person
That mysteriously becomes my own.

Ah, who knows, who knows,
If once, way back, before becoming myself,
I did not leave from such dock; if I, a ship
In the sun's slanting dawn light,
Did not depart from some other port?
Who knows if I did not leave behind,
Before this hour of the external world I see
Raying out around me,
A big dock lined with a thin crowd of people,
In a large half-awakened city,
A big mushrooming, commercial, apoplectic city,
Much as this one might be, out of Space and out of Time?

Yes, from a dock, from some sort of substantialized dock,
Real and made visible as a dock, actually a dock,
The Absolute Dock from whose unconsciously imitated pattern,
Unknowingly evoked,
We men build
Our real stone docks over real water,
Which after they're built are suddenly called
Real Things, Spirit Things, Entities in Stone Souls,
In certain moments of root feeling,
When in the outer world, as if a door were opened,
And, without anything having changed,
Everything becomes different.

Ah, the Great Dock from which we depart in Nation Ships!
The Great Original Dock, eternal and divine!
From what port? In what waters? And how is it I dream of this?
The Great Dock like other docks, but the One and Only Dock.
Like them full of the rumbling, pre-dawn silences
Blossoming into morning with the grinding of cranes
And the arrival of freight trains

E sob a nuvem negra e ocasional e leve
Do fundo das chaminés das fábricas próximas
Que lhe sombreia o chão preto de carvão pequenino que brilha,
Como se fosse a sombra duma nuvem que passasse sobre água sombria.

Ah, que essencialidade de mistério e sentido parados
Em divino êxtase revelador
Às horas cor de silêncios e angústias
Não é ponte entre qualquer cais e O Cais!

Cais negramente reflectido nas águas paradas,
Bulício a bordo dos navios,
O alma errante e instável da gente que anda embarcada,
Da gente simbólica que passa e com quem nada dura,
Que quando o navio volta ao porto
Há sempre qualquer alteração a bordo!

Ó fugas contínuas, idas, ebriedade do Diverso!
Alma eterna dos navegadores e das navegações!
Cascos reflectidos devagar nas águas,
Quando o navio larga do porto!
Flutuar como alma da vida, partir como voz,
Viver o momento trèmulamente sobre águas eternas.
Acordar para dias mais directos que os dias da Europa,
Ver portos misteriosos sobre a solidão do mar,
Virar cabos longínquos para súbitas vastas paisagens
Por inumeráveis encostas atónitas . . .

Ah, as praias longínquas, os cais vistos de longe,
E depois as praias próximas, os cais vistos de perto.
O mistério de cada ida e de cada chegada,
A dolorosa instabilidade e incompreensibilidade
Deste impossível universo
A cada hora marítima mais na própria pele sentido!
O soluço absurdo que as nossas almas derramam
Sobre as extensões de mares diferentes como ilhas ao longe,
Sobre as ilhas longínquas das costas deixadas passar,
Sobre o crescer nítido dos portos, com as suas casas o a sua gente,
Para o navio que se aproxima.

Under the occasional light black cloud
From the bowels of nearby factory chimneys
That hides the black floor of glinting coal dust
Like a cloud shadow passing over dark water.

Ah, what essence of mystery and meaning lies suspended
In the divinely revealing ecstacy
Of hours colored with silence and anxieties,
And which is no bridge from any dock to the Dock!

A dock darkly reflected in motionless waters,
The bustle on board ship,
Oh, the roving, restless soul of the boarding passengers,
The symbolic milling crowd among whom nothing abides,
And among whom, when the ship returns to port,
Some change has always occurred on board.

Oh, the continual flights and departures, drunk with Diversity,
The eternal soul of navigators and their navigations!
The hulls slowly flashing in water
As the ship takes off from port!
To float like the core of all life, to break like a voice,
To live the moment tremulously on eternal waters,
To wake up to days more direct than any in Europe,
To see mysterious ports on the wide wastes of the sea,
To round distant capes and come upon sudden vast landscapes
Past countless astonished palisades . . .

Ah, the remote beaches, the docks caught from far-off,
And then the beaches looming up, the docks seen from close-up.
The mystery of every departure and every arrival.
The sad instability, the incomprehensibility
Of this impossible universe
Felt at every maritime moment in its own skin!
The preposterous catch in the throat we feel to the core
Over the expanses of various seas with isles in the distance,
Over the far-off island coasts left behind as we pass,
Over the ports growing clearer with houses and people
As the ship approaches.

Ah, a frescura das manhãs em que se chega,
E a palidez das manhãs em que se parte,
Quando as nossas entranhas se arrepanham
E uma vaga sensação parecida com um medo
— O medo ancestral de se afastar e partir,
O misterioso receio ancestral à Chegada e ao Novo —
Encolhe-nos a pele e agonia-nos,
E todo o nosso corpo augustiado sente,
Como se fosse a nossa alma,
Uma inexplicável vontade de poder sentir isto doutra maneira:
Uma saudade a qualquer coisa,
Uma perturbação de afeições a que vaga pátria?
A que costa? a que navio? a que cais?
Que se adoece em nós o pensamento,
E só fica um grande vácuo dentro de nós,
Uma oca saciedade de minutos marítimos,
E uma ansiedade vaga que seria tédio ou dor
Se soubesse como sê-lo...

A manhã de Verão está, ainda assim, um pouco fresca.
Um leve torpor de noite anda ainda no ar sacudido.
Acelera-se ligeiramente o volante dentro de mim.
E o paquete vem entrando, porque deve vir entrando sem dúvida,
E não porque eu o veja mover-se sua distância excessiva.

Na minha imaginação ele está já perto e é visível
Em toda a extensão das linhas das suas vigias,
E treme em mim tudo, toda a carne e toda a pele,
Por causa daquela criatura que nunca chega em nenhum barco
E eu vim esperar hoje ao cais, por um mandado oblíquo.

Os navios que entram a barra,
Os navios que saem dos portos,
Os navios que passam ao longe
(Suponho-me vendo-os duma praia deserta) —
Todos estes navios abstractos quase na sua ida
Todos estes navios assim comovem-me como se fossem outra coisa
E não apenas navios, navios indo e vindo.

Ah, the morning freshness of one's arrivals
And the morning pallor of one's departures,
When the bowels tighten
And a vague sensation like fear
—The ancestral fear of moving off and leaving,
The mysterious ancestral dread of Arrival and Newness—
Shivers our hide and torments us,
And the whole of our anxious body feels,
As if it were our soul,
An inexplicable urge to be able to feel this in some other way:
Nostalgia for anything whatever—
A confused tenderness for what vague homeland?
What seacoast? what ship? what dock?
But the thought sickens us,
Leaving only a great emptiness inside us,
A hollow satiety of maritime moments
And a vague anxiety that could be tedium or sorrow
If only one knew it . . .

The Summer morning is still a bit cool,
The soft torpor of night still moves in the upcoming breeze.
The flywheel inside me moves faster, lightly,
And the steamer begins to come in, as it undoubtedly must,
And not because I see it move in from its excessive distance.

My imagination has it already nearby and visible
Through the full length of its rows of portholes,
And everything about me starts trembling, all my body and all
                                        my skin,
Because of that person who never arrives on any boat
And whom some oblique message tells me to expect today on
                                        the dock.

The ships that come in by the sandbar,
The ships that leave from the ports,
The ships that pass in the distance
(I seem to see them from a deserted beach)—
All these ships in their almost abstract passage,
All these ships move me as if they were something else
And not simply ships coming and going.

E os navios vistos de perto, mesmo que se não vá embarcar neles,
Vistos de baixo, dos botes, muralhas altas de chapas,
Vistos dentro, através das câmaras, das salas, das despensas,
Olhando de perto os mastros, afilando-se lá pró alto,
Roçando pelas cordas, descendo as escadas incómodas,
Cheirando a untada mistura metálica e marítima de tudo aquilo —
Os navios vistos de perto são outra coisa e a mesma coisa,
Dão a mesma saudade e a mesma ânsia doutra maneira.

Toda a vida marítima! tudo na vida marítima!
Insinua-se no meu sangue toda essa sedução fina
E eu cismo indeterminadamente as viagens.
Ah, as linhas das costas distantes, achatadas pelo horizonte!
Ah, os cabos, as ilhas, as praias areentas!
As solidões marítimas, como certos momentos no Pacífico
Em que náo sei por que sugestão aprendida na escola
Se sente pesar sobre os nervos o facto de que aquele é o maior
                                                    dos oceanos
E o mundo e o sabor das coisas tornam-se um deserto dentro de nós!
A extensão mais humana, mais salpicada, do Atlântico!
O Índico, o mais misterioso dos oceanos todos!
O Mediterrâneo, doce, sem mistério nenhum, clássico, um mar para bate
De encontro a esplanadas olhadas de jardins próximos por
                                                    estátuas brancas!
Todos os mares, todos os estreitos, todas as baías, todos os golfos,
Queria apertá-los ao peito, senti-los bem e morrer!

E vós, ó coisas navais, meus velhos brinquedos de sonho!
Componde fora de mim a minha vida interior!
Quilhas, mastros e velas, rodas do leme, cordagens,
Chaminés de vapores, hélices, gáveas, flâmulas,
Galdropes, escotilhas, caldeiras, colectores, válvulas;
Caí por mim dentro em montão, em monte,
Como o conteúdo confuso de uma gaveta despejada no chão!
Sede vós o tesouro da minha avareza febril,
Sede vós os frutos da árvore da minha imaginação,
Tema de cantos meus, sangue nas veias da minha inteligência,

And the ships seen from up close, even when one doesn't board
them,
Seen from below and from rowboats, with high iron sides,
Seen inside, through the state rooms, dining rooms, holds,
Seeing the masts from up close, pointing way up,
Leaping through cordage, stepping down clumsy gangways,
Smelling the oily, metallic sea mixture of it all—
The ships seen close by are something else and the same,
Stirring the same nostalgia and the same hankering for something
else.

All seafaring life! Anything to do with seafaring life!
All that fine seductiveness of the sea enters my blood
And I dream indeterminately of voyages.
Ah, the far-away coastlines, flattened on the horizon!
Ah, the capes, the islands, the sandy beaches!
The oceanic solitudes, like certain moments on the Pacific
When, I do not know by what suggestion picked up at school,
One feels dragging at one's nerves the fact that this is the biggest
ocean,
And the whole world and the taste of everything becomes a
wasteland inside us!
The more human, more splashing expanse of the Atlantic!
The Indian, most mysterious ocean of all!
The sweet Mediterranean, with nothing mysterious about it, oh
classical sea dashing
Up the esplanades seen by white statues from nearby gardens!
All seas, all straits, all bays, all gulfs—
I'd like to clutch them to my breast, feel them in my arms, and die!

And all you seafaring things, my old dream playthings,
Compose beyond me my inner life!
Keels, masts, and sails, helm wheels, ropes,
The funnels of steamers, propellers, topsails, pennants,
Tiller ropes, hatchways, boilers, engine-sumps, valves—
Fall through me in a heap, in a mountain,
Like the mixed contents of a locker littered on the floor!
Be the hoard of my febrile avarice,
Be the fruits of the tree of my imagination,
The theme of my songs, the blood of my veined intelligence,

Vosso seja o laço que me une ao exterior pela estética,
Fornecei-me metáforas imagens, literatura,
Porque em real verdade, a sério, literalmente,
Minhas sensações são um barco de quilha pró ar,
Minha imaginação uma âncora meio submersa,
Minha ânsia um remo partido,
E a tessitura dos meus nervos uma rede a secar na praia!

Soa no acaso do rio um apito, só um.
Treme já todo o chão do meu psiquismo.
Acelera-se cada vez mais o volante dentro de mim.

Ah, os paquetes, as viagens, a não-se-saber-a-paradeiro
De Fulano-de-tal, marítimo, nosso conhecido!
Ah, a glória de se saber que um homem que andava connosco
Morreu afogado ao pé duma ilha do Pacífico!
Nós que andámos com ele vamos falar nisso a todos.
Com um orgulho legítimo, com uma confiança invisível
Em que tudo isso tenha um sentido mais belo e mais vasto
Que apenas o ter-se perdido o barco onde ele ia
E ele ter ido ao fundo por lhe ter entrado água prós pulmões!

Ah, os paquetes, os navios-carvoeiros, os navios de vela!
Vão rareando — ai de mim! — os navios de vela nos mares!

Eu o engenheiro, eu o civilizado, eu o educado no esthangeiro,
                                              as máquinas
Eu o engenheiro, eu o civilizado, eu o educado no esthangeiro,
Gostaria de ter outra vez ao pé da minha vista só veleiros e
                                              barcos de madeira.
De não saber doutra vida marítima que a antiga vida dos mares!
Porque os mares antigos são a Distância Absoluta,
O Puro Longe, liberto do peso do Actual...
E ah, como aqui tudo me lembra essa vida melhor,
Esses mares, maiores, porque se navegava mais devagar.
Esses mares, misteriosos, porque se sabia menos deles.

Let yours be the thread of esthetics that binds me to external things,
Give me metaphors, images, literature,
Because in actual fact, seriously, literally,
My sensations are a ship with its keel in the wind,
My imagination a half-sunken anchor,
My anxiety a broken oar,
And the weave of my nerves a net to dry on a beach!

Just by chance, a whistle sounds off the river—only one.
Now the base of my whole psychic system is trembling.
The flywheel inside me whirs faster and faster.

Ah, the steamers, the voyages off to I don't know what places
Of old So-and-So, the sailor, our old friend!
Ah, the glory of knowing that a man who used to walk here
                                        beside me
Was drowned off an island in the Pacific!
We who go on walking as he did will now discuss it with everyone,
With legitimate pride, an impalpable conviction
That all this has a finer, a vaster meaning
Than even the loss of the ship where he went down,
Went down to the bottom because water got into his lungs!

Ah, the steamers, the merchant ships, the schooners!
The sailing ships—alas!—becoming rarer on the high seas!

And I, who love modern civilizatons, I who embrace the machine
                                        with all my heart,
I, the engineer, the civilized mind, the man educated abroad,
I would like to see nothing before me but schooners and ships
                                        built of timber,
And hear of no other maritime life than the old seafaring life!
Because the ancient seas are Absolute Distance,
Pure Extension, free of the weight of Actuality . . .
Ah, how everything here reminds me of that better life,
Of those seas that were vaster because sailed more slowly,
Of those seas more mysterious because so little was known
                                        about them.

Todo o vapor ao longe é um barco de vela perto.
Todo o navio disante visto agora é um navio no passado visto próximo.
Todos os marinheiros invisíveis a bordo dos navios no horizonte
São os marinheiros visíveis do tempo dos velhos navios,
Da época lenta e veleira das navegações perigosas,
Da época de madeira e lona das viagens que duravam meses.

Toma-me pouco a pouco o delírio das coisas marítimas,
Penetram-me fisicamente o cais e a sua atmosfera,
O marulho do Tejo galga-me por cima dos sentidos,
E começo a sonhar, começo a envolver-me do sonho das águas,
Começam a pegar bem as correias-de-transmissão na minh'alma
E a aceleração do volante sacode-me nìtidamente.

Chamam por mim as águas,
Chamam por mim os mares,
Chamam por mim, levantando uma voz corpórea, os longes,
As épocas marítimas todas sentidas no passado, a chamar.

Tu, marinheiro inglês, Jim Barns meu amigo, foste tu
Que me ensinaste esse grito antiquíssimo, inglês,
Que tão venenosamente resume
Para as almas complexas como a minha
O chamamento confuso das águas,
A voz inédita e implicita de todas as coisas do mar,
Dos naufrágios, das viagens longínquas, das travessias perigosas.
Esse teu grito inglês, tornado universal no meu sangue,
Sem feitio de grito, sem forma humana nem voz.
Esse grito tremendo que parece soar
De dentro duma caverna cuja abóbada é o céu
E parece narrar todas as sinistras coisas
Que podem acontecer no Longe, no Mar, pela Noite . . .
(Fingias sempre que era por uma escuna que chamavas,
E dizias assim, pondo uma mão de cada lado da boca,
Fazendo porta-voz das grandes mãos curtidas e escuras:

Ahò-ò-ò ·ò-ò-ò-ò-ò-ò-ò-ò — yyyy . . .
Schooner ahò-ò-ò-ò-ò-ò-ò-ò-ò-ò-ò-ò-ò — yyyy . . .)

From far off each steamer is a sailing ship nearby,
Each ship seen from afar now, is a ship seen up close in the past. .
All the invisible sailors aboard ships on the horizon
Are the visible sailors back in the time of sailing ships,
Back in the slow-moving sailing age of dangerous voyages,
Back in the age of canvas and timbers and of voyages that took
months.

Little by little the spell of seagoing things comes over me.
The dock and its ambience penetrate me physically,
The tide of the Tagus floods all my senses
And I start dreaming, I start wrapping myself up in a dream of
waters,
Driving-belts start winding themselves firmly around my soul,
And the fast-whirring flywheel clearly shakes me.

Waters are calling me.
Seas are calling me.
All distances raise a bodily voice and call me,
And all maritime ages known in the past are calling me.

It was you, Jim Barnes, my friend, the English sailor, it was you
Who taught me that ageless English shout,
Which for such complex souls as mine
So venomously sums up
The confused cry of the waters,
The implicit, unrecordable voice of everything at sea,
The shipwrecks, the endless voyages, the hazardous crossings,
That English shout of yours, universalized in my blood,
Like no other shout, without human form or voice,
That tremendous cry that seems to resound
Inside a cave whose vault is the sky
And telling of all the sinister things
That might occur Out There, in the Sea, at Night . . .
(You always pretended it was a schooner you were calling,
And as you said it, cupping a hand at either side of your mouth,
Making a megaphone out of your big dark tawny hands:

Ahó-ó-ó-o-o-o-o-o-o-o—yyyy . . .
Schooner ahó-ó-ó-o-o-o-o-o-o-o-o-o-o-o-o—yyyy . . .)

Escuto-te de aqui, agora, e deperto a qualquer coisa.
Estremece o vento. Sobe a manhã. O calor abre.
Sinto corarem-me as faces.
Meus olhos conscientes dilatam-se.
O êxtase em mim levanta-se, cresce, avança,
E com um ruído cego de arruaça, acentua-se
O giro vivo do volante.

Ó clamoroso chamamento
A cujo calor, a cuja fúria fervem em mim
Numa unidade explosiva todas as minhas ânsias,
Meus próprios tédios tornados dinâmicos, todos!...
Apelo lançado ao meu sangue
Dum amor passado, não sei onde, que volve
E ainda tem força para me atrair e puxar,
Que ainda tem força para me fazer odiar esta vida
Que passo entre a impenetrabilidade física e psíquica
Do gente real com que vivo!

Ah seja como for, seja por onde for, partir!
Largar por aí fora, pelas ondas, pelo perigo, pelo mar.
Ir para Longe, ir para Fora, para a Distância Abstracta,
Indefinidamente, pelas noites misteriosas e fundas,
Levado, como a poeira, plos ventos, plos vendavais!
Ir, ir, ir, ir de vez!

Todo o meu sangue raiva por asas!
Todo o meu corpo atira-se prá frente!
Galgo pla minha imaginação fora em torrentes!
Atropelo-me, rujo, precipito-me!...
Estoiram em espuma as minhas ânsias
E a minha carne é uma onda dando de econtro a rochedos!

Pensando nisto — ó raiva! pensando nisto — ó fúria!
Pensando nesta estreiteza da minha vida cheia de ânsias,
Sùbitamente, trèmulamente, extraorbitadamente,
Com uma oscilação viciosa, vasta, violenta,
Do volante vivo da minha imaginação,

I listen to you, here and now, and am alert to everything.
The wind trembles. The morning rises. The heat begins.
I feel my cheeks redden.
My conscious eyes dilate.
An ecstasy rises in me, spreads, goes forth,
And with a blind upsurge of feeling the living flywheel
In me keeps time with it.

Oh clamorous outcry,
Your heat and fury bring boiling up inside me
All my fears in one explosive unity,
All my boredom turns dynamic, every bit of it! . . .
A cry hurled at my blood
From some past love, out of where I do not know,
But coming back and still with power to attract and to repel me,
Still with power to make me hate this life
I spend of physical and psychic impenetrability
Among the real people I live with!

Ah, just to get away, I don't care how or where!
Just to take to the high seas, through perilous waves and oceans,
To be off toward the Far Away, to Outer Space, to Abstract
                                                    Distance,
Indefinitely, through deep mysterious nights,
Carried like dust by winds, by gales!
Moving, moving, moving, again and again!

All my blood rages for wings!
My whole body shoots on ahead!
My imagination rushes out through torrents,
I trample over myself, roaring, throwing myself down into it! . . .
My anxieties explode in foam
Where my flesh is a wave setting out to break against rocks!

As I think of this—o madness!—as I think of this, o fury!
Thinking of my straight-and-narrow life, full of feverish desires,
Suddenly, tremulously, extraorbitally,
With one viciously vast and violent twist
Of the living flywheel of my imagination,

Rompe, por mim, assobiando, silvando, vertiginando,
O cio sombrio e sádico da estrídula vida marítima.

Eh marinheiros, gajeiros! eh tripulantes, pilotos!
Navegadores, mareantes, marujos, aventureiros!
Eh capitães de navios! homens ao leme e em mastros!
Homens que dormem em beliches rudes!
Homens que dormem co'o Perigo a espreitar plas vigias!
Homens que dormem co'a Morte por travesseiro!
Homens que têm tombadilhos, que têm pontes donde olhar
A imensidade imensa do mar imenso!
Eh manipuladores dos guindastes de carga!
Eh amainadores de velas, fogueiros, criados de bordo!

Homens que metem a carga nos porões!
Homens que enrolam cabos no convés!
Homens que limpam os metais das escotilhas!
Homens do leme! homens das máquinas! homens dos mastros!
Eh-eh-eh-eh-eh-eh-eh!
Gente de boné de pala! Gente de camisola de malha!
Gente de âncoras e bandeiras cruzadas bordadas no peito!
Gente tatuada! gente de cachimbo! gente de amurada!
Gente escura de tanto sol, crestada de tanta chuva,
Limpa de olhos de tanta imensidade diante deles,
Audaz de rosto de tanto ventos que lhes bateram a valer!

Eh-eh-eh-eh-eh-eh-eh!
Homens que vistes a Patagónia!
Homens que passastes pela Austrália!
Que enchestes o vosso olhar de costas que nunca verei!
Que fostes a terra em terras onde nunca descerei!
Que comprastes artigos toscos em colónias à proa de sertões!
E fizestes tudo isso como se não fosse nada,
Como se isso fosse natural,
Como se a vida fosse isso,
Como nem sequer cumprindo um destino!
Eh-eh-eh-eh-eh-eh-eh!
Homens do mar actual! homens do mar passado!
Comissários de bordo! escravos das galés! combatentes de Lepanto!

There breaks through me, whistling, trilling and whirling,
This somber, sadistic envy of all strident seafaring life.

Hey there, sailors, topsmen! Hey, crewmen, pilots!
Navigators, mariners, seamen, adventurers!
Hey, ships' captains! Men at the helm and the masts!
Men asleep in their crude bunks!
Men sleeping with Danger and keeping the watches!
Men sleeping with Death for a whole crossing!
Men standing on decks, standing on bridges looking out on
The immense immensity of the immense ocean!
Hey there, you winch-crane operators!
You furlers of sail, stokers and stewards!

Men who load cargo in the holds!
Men who coil ropes on deck!
Men who wash down the hatchways!
Men at the helm, men at the machines, men at the masts!
Hey there, hey there, hey there!
Men in peaked caps! Men in mesh undershirts!
Men with anchors and crossed pennants decorating their chests!
Tattooed men! Men with pipes!
Men darkened by so much sun, blasted by so much rain,
Made sharp-eyed by so much immensity before them,
Tough-looking because of all the winds they stood up to!

Hey there, hey there, hey!
Men who saw Patagonia!
Men who shipped out to Australia!
Men whose eyes filled with shores I'll never see!
Who made for land in places where I'll never set foot!
Who bought crude goods from the natives in the hinterland
                                            stations!
And who did it all as though it were a matter of course,
As though it were all natural,
As though that's what life was like,
As though they weren't even fulfilling a destiny!
Hey, hey, hey, hey, hey, hey!
Men of the modern seas, men of the ancient seas!
Pursers! Galley slaves! Men fighting in Lepanto!

Pirates do tempo de Roma! Navegadores da Grécia!
Fenícios! Cartagineses! Portugueses atirados de Sagres
Para a aventura indefinida, para o Mar Absoluto, para realizar
                                        o Impossível!
Eh-eh-eh-eh-eh-eh-eh-eh-eh!
Homens que erguestes padrões, que destes nomes a cabos!
Homens que negociastes pela primeira vez com pretos!
Que primerio vendestes escravos de novas terras!
Que destes o primeiro espasmo europeu às negras atónitas!
Que trouxestes ouro, missanga, madeiras cheirosas, setas,
De encostas explodindo em verde vegetação!
Homens que saqueastes tranquilas povoações africanas,
Que fizistes fugir com o ruído de canhões essas raças,
Que matastes, roubastes, torturastes, ganhastes
Os prémios de Novidade de quem, de cabeça baixa
Arremete contra o mistério de novos mares! Eh-eh-eh-eh-eh!
A vós todos num, a vós todos em vós todos como um,
A vós todos misturados, entrecruzados.
A vós todos sangrentos, violentos, odiados, temidos, sagrados,
Eu vos saúdo, eu vos saúdo, eu vos saúdo!
Eh-eh-eh-eh eh! Eh eh-eh-eh eh! Eh-eh-eh eh-eh-eh eh!
Eh lahô-lahô loHO-lahá-á-á-à-à!

Quero ir convosco, quero ir convosco,
Ao mesmo tempo com vós todos
Pra toda a parte pr'onde fostes!
Quero encontrar vossos perigos frente a frente,
Sentir na minha cara os ventos que engelharam as vossas,
Cuspir dos lábios o sal dos mares que beijaram os vossos,
Ter braços na vossa faina, partilhar das vossas tormentas,
Chegar como vós, enfim, a extraordinários portos!
Fugir convosco à civilização!
Perder convosco a noção da moral!
Sentir mudar-se no longe a minha humanidade!
Beber convosco em mares do sul
Novas selvajarias, novas balbúrdias da alma,
Novos fogos centrais no meu vulcânico espírito!
Ir convosco, despir de mim — ah! põe-te daqui pra fora! —

Pirates in Roman times! Greek navigators!
Phoenicians, Carthaginians, Portuguese hurled out of Sagres
To boundless adventure on the Absolute Sea to realize the
                                                 Impossible!
Hey there, hey there, hey . . .
You men who raised stone pillars to mark the coasts you discovered
                                        and named the capes!
Who first traded with the Negroes!
Who first sold slaves from new lands!
Who gave the astonished Negresses their first European orgasm!
You who brought back gold, glass beads, fragrant woods, arrows,
From coasts exploding with green vegetation!
You men who plundered peaceful African villages,
Scattering the natives with the roar of your cannon,
You who murdered, robbed, tortured, and grabbed the reward
Of the New Thing promised to those who lowered their heads
To rush out against the mystery of the new seas! Hey, hey, hey!
To all of you together, to all of you as though you were one,
To all of you mixed together and interlocking,
To all of you bloody, violent, hated, feared, revered,
I salute you, I salute you, I salute you!
Hey, hey, hey! Hey, hey, hey! Hey, hey, hey!
Hello there, hello there, hello, he . . . lloo . . . ooo!

I want to take off with you, I want to go away with you,
With all of you at once,
To every place you went!
I want to meet the dangers you knew face to face,
To feel across my cheeks the winds that wrinkled yours,
To spit the salt sea that kissed your lips,
To pitch in with you as you work, to share the storms with you,
To reach like you, at last, extraordinary ports!
To flee with you from civilization!
To lose with you all moral sense!
To feel my humanity back off, silenced!
To drink with you in southern seas
New savageries, new tumults of the heart,
New central fires in my volcanic spirit!
To take off with you and leave behind—ah, come now, get in
                                                 front of me!

O meu traje de civilizado, a minha brandura de acções,
Meu medo inato das cadeias
Minha pacífica vida,
A minha vida sentada, estática, regrada e revista!

No mar, no mar, no mar, no mar,
Eh! pôr no mar, ao vento, às vagas,
A minha vida!
Salgar de espuma arremessada pelos ventos
Meu paladar das grandes viagens.
Fustigar de água chicoteante as carnes da minha aventura,
Repassar de frios oceânicos os ossos da minha existência,
Flagelar, cortar, engelhar de ventos, de espumas, de sóis,
Meu ser ciclónico e atlântico,
Meus nervos postos como enxárcias,
Lira nas mãos dos ventos!

Sim, sim, sim... Crucificai-me nas navegações
E as minhas espáduas gozarão a minha cruz!
Atai-me as viagens como a postes
E a sensação dos postes entrará pela minha espinha
E eu passarei a senti-los num vasto espasmo passivo!
Fazei o que quiserdes de mim, logo que seja nos mares,
Sobre conveses, ao som de vagas,
Que me rasgueis, mateis, firais!
O que quero é levar prá Morte
Uma alma a transbordar de Mar,
Ébria a cair das coisas marítimas,
Tanto dos marujos como das âncoras, dos cabos,
Tanto das costas longínquas como do ruído dos ventos,
Tanto do Longe como do Cais, tanto dos naufrágios
Como dos tranquilos comércios,
Tanto dos mastros como das vagas,
Levar prá Morte com dor, voluptuosamente,
Um copo cheio de sanguessugas, a sugar, a sugar,
De estranhas verdes absurdas sanguessugas marítimas!

Façam enxárcias das minhas veias!
Amarras dos meus músculos!
Arranquem-me a pele, preguem-a às quilhas.

—My civilized suit, my genteel behavior,
My innate fear of jails,
My peaceful life,
My sedentary, static, orderly, self-disciplined life!

To sea, to sea, to sea, to sea,
Hey there! Put to sea, with the winds and the waves,
Oh my life!
With the foam on the winds
To salten my taste for great voyages,
With lashing torrents to whip my flesh to adventure,
Soak the bones of existence in freezing seas,
Flagellate, cut, and wrinkle with wind, sun, and foam
My cyclonic Atlantic being,
My nerves spread out like shroud ropes,
A harp in the hands of the winds!

Yes, yes, yes . . . Crucify me as you sail
And my shoulders will love the weight of the cross!
Bind me to each voyage as to a stake
And the pressure of the stake will pierce my spine
Till I feel it in one great passive orgasm!
Do what you want with me, so long as it's done at sea,
On deck, on top of the waves,
Wound me, kill me, tear me apart!
What I'd like is to bring to Death
A soul transformed by the Sea,
Dead drunk on everything having to do with the sea,
With sailors as much as with anchors and capes,
With far-away coasts as much as with wind sounds,
With the Distant as with the Dock, with shipwrecks
As with run-of-the-mill shipping,
With masts as with waves,
And in voluptuous mourning, bring Death
A body swarming with leeches, sucking, sucking—
Those strange green absurd sea leeches!

Make shroud ropes out of my veins!
Hawsers out of muscles!
Tear off my skin, nail it down to the keels,

E possa eu sentir a dor dos pregos e nunca deixar de sentir!
Façam do meu coração uma flâmula de almirante
Na hora de guerra dos velhos navios!

Calquem aos pés nos conveses meus olhos arrancados!
Quebrem-me os ossos de encontro às amuradas!
Fustiguem-me atado aos mastros, fustiguem-me!
A todos os ventos de todas as latitudes e longitudes
Derramem meu sangue sobre as águas arremessadas
Que atravessam o navio, o tombadilho, de lado a lado.
Nas vascas bravas das tormentas!

Ter a audácia ao vento dos panos das velas!
Ser, como as gáveas altas, o assobio dos ventos!
A velha guitarra do Fado dos mares cheios de perigos,
Canção para os navegadores ouvirem e não repetirem!

Os marinheiros que se sublevaram
Enforcaram o capitão numa verga.
Desembarcaram um outro numa ilha deserta.
Marooned!
O sol dos trópicos pôs a febre da pirataria antiga
Nas minhas veias intensivas.
Os ventos da Patagónia tatuaram a minha imaginação
De imagens trágicas e obscenas.
Fogo, fogo, fogo, dentro de mim!
Sangue! sangue! sangue! sangue!
Explode todo o meu cérebro!
Parte-se-me o mundo em vermelho!
Estoiram-me com o som de amarras as veias!
E estala em mim, feroz, voraz,
A canção do Grande Pirata,
A morte berrada do Grande Pirata a cantar
Até meter pavor plas espinhas dos seus homens abaixo.
Lá da ré a morrer, e a berrar, a cantar!

Fifteen men on the Dead Man's Chest.
Yo-ho ho and a bottle of rum!

Let me feel the pain of the nails and never stop feeling it!
Out of my heart make an admiral's flag
Unfurled in a battle between old sailing ships!

Let my ripped-out eyes be squashed underfoot on the decks!
Break my bones against hulls!
Tie me to masts and lash me, lash me!
Let the winds of all latitudes, longitudes,
Spread my blood over rushing waters
That dash side to side across poop decks
In the gale's rough caterwauling!

To be daring as cloth sails taut in the wind!
Like the high topsails in the whistling winds!
The old guitar, strumming a *fado* all about the perils at sea;
A song for sailors to hear and never repeat!

The sailors who mutinied
Have hanged their captain from a yardarm.
Another they've left stranded on a deserted island.
Marooned!
The tropical sun has put the old pirate fever
In my burning veins.
The winds of Patagonia have tattooed on my imagination
Obscene and tragic images.
Fire, fire, oh fire inside me!
Blood, blood, blood, blood!
My skull explodes!
My world comes apart in crimson hunks,
My veins snap like clanking chains,
And out of me, fierce and voracious, bursts
The Great Pirate song,
The Great Pirate bellowing out this death knell,
His men below quaking with fear in their backbones,
And there on the quarterdeck amid the dying and shrieking, the
                                                          singing:

> *Fifteen men on a Dead Man's Chest.*
> *Yo-ho—ho and a bottle of rum!*

E depois a gritar, numa voz já irreal, a estoirar no ar:

Darby M'Graw-aw-aw-aw-aw!
Darby M'Graw-aw-aw-aw-aw-aw-aw-aw!
Fetch a-a-aft the ru-u-u-u-u-u-u-u-um, Darby,

Eia, que vida essa! essa era a vida, eia!
Eh-eh-eh-eh-eh-eh-eh!
Eh-lahô-lahô-laHO-lahá-á-á-à-à!
Eh-eh-eh-eh-eh-eh-eh!

Quilhas partidas, navios ao fundo, sangue nos mares
Conveses cheios de sangue, fragmentos de corpos!
Dedos decepados sobre amuradas!
Cabeças de crianças, aqui, acolá!
Gente de olhos fora, a gritar, a uivar!
Eh-eh-eh-eh-eh-eh-eh-eh-eh-eh!
Eh-eh-eh-eh-eh-eh-eh-eh-eh-eh!
Embrulho-me em tudo isto como uma capa no frio!
Roço-me por tudo isto como uma gata com cio por um muro!
Rujo como um leão faminto para tudo isto!
Arremeto como um toiro louco sobre tudo isto!
Cravo unhas, parto garras, sangro dos dentes sobre isto!
Eh-eh-eh-eh-eh-eh-eh-eh-eh-eh!

De repente estala-me sobre os ouvidos
Como um clarim a meu lado,
O velho grito, mas agora irado, metálico,
Chamando a presa que se avista,
A escuna que vai ser tomada:

Ahó-ó-ó-ó-ó-ó-ó-ó-ó-ó-ó — yyyy...
Schooner ahó-ó-ó-ó-ó-ó-ó-ó-ó-ó-ó-ó-ó-ó — yyyy...

O mundo inteiro não existe para mim! Ardo vermelho!
Rujo na fúria da abordagem!
Pirata-mor! César-Pirata!
Pilho, mato, esfacelo, rasgo!

Só sinto o mar, a presa, o saque!
Só sinto em mim bater, baterem-me

Then the scream, in a voice grown unreal, shatters the air:

> *Darby M'Graw-aw-aw-aw-aw!*
> *Darby M'Graw-aw-aw-aw-aw-aw-aw-aw!*
> *Fetch a-a-aft the ru-u-u-u-u-u-u-u-um, Darby!*

Hey, that's the life, that was the life, ho! ho!
Ha-ha! ho-ho! ha-ha!
Hey there, hey there, that's it!

Crushed keels, sunk ships, blood on the waters,
Decks floating in gore, chunks of corpses!
Fingers lopped off on the gunwales!
Here and there, the heads of infants!
People with eyes gouged out screaming and howling!
Hey, that's it, hey, hey, hey!
Hey, that's it, hey, hey, hey!
I'm wrapped up in all this like a cape against the cold!
I rub up against all this like a cat in heat against the wall!
I roar through it all like a hungry lion!
I rush through it all like a mad bull!
I sink my nails, I tear my claws, I bloody my teeth through it all!
Hey, that's it, ho-ho, that's it!

My ears suddenly split—
It's like a great trumpet there at my side—
With that old cry, but raging, metallic now,
Calling out for its prize to show itself,
The schooner about to be taken:

> *Aho-o-o-o-o-o-o-o-o-o . . . yyy!*
> *Schooner aho-o-o-o-o-o-o-o-o-o . . . yyy!*

For me the whole world comes to a stop. I'm red hot!
I roar in a frenzy to board her!
The Pirate Chief! King of the Pirates!
I pillage, I kill, I tear, I cut everything up!

All I feel is the sea—the seizure, the looting!
All I feel is the tom-tom of veins beating in me,

As veias das minhas fontes!
Escorre sangue quente a minha sensação dos meus olhos!
Eh-eh-eh-eh-eh-eh-eh-eh-eh-eh-eh!

Ah piratas, piratas, piratas!
Piratas, amai-me e odiai-me!
Misturai-me convosco, piratas!

Vossa fúria, vossa crueldade como falam ao sangue
Dum corpo de mulher que foi meu outrora e cujo cio sobrevive!

Eu queria ser um bicho representativo de todos os vossos gestos,
Um bicho que cravasse dentes nas amuradas, nas quilhas
Que comesse mastros, bebesse sangue e alcatrão nos conveses,
Trincasse velas, remos, cordame e poleame,
Serpente do mar feminina e monstruosa cevando-se nos crimes!

E há uma sinfonia de sensações incompatíveis e análogas.
Há uma orquestração no meu sangue de balbúrdias de crimes.
De estrépitos espasmados de orgias de sangue nos mares,
Furibundamente, como um vendaval de calor pelo espírito,
Nuvem de poeira quente anuviando a minha lucidez
E fazendo-me ver e sonhar isto tudo só com a pele e as veias!

Os pirates, a pirataria, os barcos, a hora,
Aquela hora marítima em que as presas são assaltadas,
E o terror dos apresados foge prá loucura — essa hora,
No seu total de crimes, terror, barcos, gente, mar, céu, nuvens,
Brisa, latitude, longitude, vozearia,
Queria eu que fosse em seu Todo meu corpo em seu Todo, sofrendo,
Que fosse meu corpo e meu sangue, compusesse meu ser em vermelho,
Florescesse como uma ferida comichando na carne irreal da minha alm

Ah, ser tudo nos crimes! ser todos os elementos componentes
Dos assaltos aos barcos e das chacinas e das violações!
Ser quanto foi no lugar dos saques!
Ser quanto viveu ou jazeu no local das tragédias de sangue!
Ser o pirata-resumo de toda, a pirataria no seu auge,
E a vítama-síntese, mas de carne e osso, de todos os piratas do mundo

Beating my temples!
Hot blood drains out the sensation of having two eyes!
Hey-hey, that's it, that's it! Hey-hey-hey!

Ah, pirates, pirates, pirates!
Love me and hate me, pirates!
Pirates, let me melt into you!

Your cruel fury speaks to my blood
Of a woman's body that once was my own
And of which nothing is left but the sexual itch!

I want to be the beast
That acts out all your gestures,
That sinks its teeth in keels and gunwales,
That eats the masts and sops up blood and tar on deck,
That chews up sails and oars, ropes and pulleys.
A monster female sea-serpent, glutting herself on crimes!

A symphony of sensations rises, incompatible and analogous,
An orchestration of tumultuous crimes, dinning in my blood,
Of spasmodic bloody orgies resounding on the sea,
Rising wildly like a hot gale in my soul,
A hot dust cloud dimming my lucidity,
Making me see and dream all this through my skin and veins only!

Pirates and piracy, ships and the moment,
That maritime moment when the prize is boarded
And the prisoners' terror approaches madness—that moment
With all its crimes, horror, ships, people, sea, sky, clouds,
Winds, latitude and longitude, outcries—
How I wish that in its allness it was my body in its allness, suffering,
My body and my blood, my whole being made one livid crimson glob
In bloom, like an itching wound, in the unreal flesh of my soul!

To be all those crimes! to be part and parcel
Of all those raids on ships, the massacres, the rapes!
To be all that happened where the plunder was!
To be all that lived or died where the bloody tragedies took place!
To be the grand-sum-total-pirate of piracy at its height,
And the grand-sum-total-victim, flesh and bone, of all the pirates
                                        in the world!

Ser o meu corpo passivo a mulher-todas-as-mulheres
Que foram violadas, mortas, feridas, rasgadas pelos piratas!
Ser no meu ser subjugado a fêmea que tem de ser deles
E sentir tudo isso — todas estas coisas duma só vez — pela espinha!

Ó meus peludos e rudes heróis da aventura e do crime!
Minhas marítimas feras, maridos da minha imaginação!
Amantes casuais da obliquidade das minhas sensações!
Queria ser Aquela que vos esperasse nos portos,
A vós, odiados amados do seu sangue de pirata nos sonhos!
Porque ela teria convosco, mas só em espírito, raivado
Sobre os cadáveres nus das vítimas que fazeis no mar!
Porque ela teria acompanhado vosso crime, e na orgia oceânica
Seu espírito de bruxa dançaria invisível em volta dos gestos
Dos vossos corpos, dos vossos cutelos, das vossas mãos estranguladoras!
E ela em terra, esperando-vos, quando viésseis, se acaso viésseis,
Iria beber nos rugidos do vosso amor todo o vasto,
Todo o nevoento e sinistro perfume das vossas vitórias,
E através dos vossos espasmos silvaria um sabbat de vermelho e amare
A carne rasgada, a carne aberta e estripada, o sangue correndo!
Agora, no ague conciso de sonhar o que vós fazíeis,
Perco-me todo de mim, já não vos pertenço, sou vós,
A minha feminidade que vos acompanha é ser as vossas almas!
Estar por dentro de toda a vossa ferocidade, quando a praticáveis!
Sugar por dentro a vosso consciência das vossas sensações
Quando tingíeis de sangue os mares altos,
Quando de vez em quando atiráveis aos tubarões
Os corpos vivos ainda dos feridos, a carne rosada das crianças
E leváveis as mães às amuradas para verem o que lhes acontecia!

Estar convosco na carnagem, na pilhagem!
Estar orquestrado convosco na sinfonia dos saques!
Ah, não sei quê, não sei quanto queria eu ser de vós!
Não era só ser-vos a fêmea, ser-vos as fêmeas, ser-vos vítimas,
Ser-vos as vítimas — homens, mulheres,crianças, navios —,
Não era só ser a hora e os barcos e as ondas,

Let my passive body be the grand-sum-total-woman of all women
Who were raped, killed, wounded, torn apart by pirates!
Let my violated body be that woman's who must serve them all!
And feel it all—feel all these things at once—in my backbone!

Oh, my heroes, coarse and hairy, adventurous and criminal!
My seafaring beasts, you husbands of my brain!
Quick lovers of my oblique sensations!
I'd love to be your One-and-Only awaiting you in every port,
You, the loved-and-hated pirates of her dreams!
Because she would be with you, though only in spirit, raped
Along with the naked corpses of your victims at sea!
Because she would be your accomplice in crime and in your oceanic
                                          orgies,
Her witch's spirit dancing invisibly amid the movements
Of your bodies, amid your cutlasses and your stranglers' hands!
And she, back on land, awaiting your return, if return you will,
She would drink in your roaring love, all the vast wide-openness,
All the fog-filled, sinister fragrance of your conquests,
And during your orgasms she'd whistle the red-yellow *sabbath* of
                                          a black mass!
Flesh torn, ripped open, disembowled, the blood pouring out,
Now, at the peak of my dream of your exploits,
I am totally lost; no longer belonging to you, I *am* you,
My femininity, which accompanied you, become your very soul!
Now to be inside all your ferocity when you practice it,
Absorbing from within the feel of your sensations
When you stain the high seas with blood,
When occasionally you toss to the sharks
The still-living bodies of the wounded, the rosy flesh of children,
And drag their mothers to the gunwales to watch it happening!

To be with you at the carnage and pillaging!
To be attuned to the symphony of your plundering!
Ah, I can't say, I can't tell you how much, I'd love to be with you!
Not just be there as your woman, be all women for you, be all your
                                          victims,
Being each and all victims—men, women, children, ships—
And not just be your opportune moment aboard ship and the waves,

Não era só ser vossas almas, vossos corpos, vossa fúria, vossa posse,
Não era só ser concretamente vosso acto abstracto de orgia,
Não era só isto que eu queria ser — era mais que isto o Deus-isto!
Era preciso ser Deus, o Deus dum culto ao contrário,
Um Deus monstruoso e satânico, um Deus dum panteísmo de sangue,
Para poder encher toda a medida da minha fúria imaginativa,
Para poder nunca esgotar os meus desejos de identidade
Com o cada, e o tudo, e o mais-que-tudo das vossas vitórias!

Ah, torturai-me para me curardes!
Minha carne — fazei dela o ar que os vossos cutelos atravessam
Antes de caírem sobre as cabeças e os ombros!
Minhas veias sejam os fatos que as facas trespassam!
Minha imaginação o corpo das mulheres que violais!
Minha inteligência o convés onde estais de pé matando!
Minha vida toda, no seu conjunto nervoso, histérico, absurdo,
O grande organismo de que cada acto de pirataria que se cometeu
Fosse uma célula consciente — e todo eu turbilhonasse
Como uma imensa podridão ondeando, e fosse aquilo tudo!

Com tal velocidade desmedida, pavorosa,
A máquina de febre das minhas visões transbordantes
Gira agora que a minha consciência, volante,
É apenas um nevoento círculo assobiando no ar.

> *Fifteen men on the Dead Man's Chest.*
> *Yo-ho ho and a bottle of rum!*

Eh-lahô-lahô-laHO — lahá-á-ááá — ààà . . .

Ah! a selvajaria desta selvajaria! Merda
Pra toda a vida como a nossa, que não é nada disto!
Eu pr'àqui engenheiro, prático à força, sensível a tudo,
Pr'àqui parado, em relação a vós, mesmo quando ando;
Mesmo quando ajo, inerte; mesmo quando me imponho, débil;
Estático, quebrado, dissidente cobarde da vossa Glória,

Not just your souls, your bodies, your fury, your booty,
Not just being concretely your abstract orgiastic acts,
It's not just this that I want to be but, more than all this, be
                              God of such Thisness!
I'd have to be God, I'd have to be God of some opposing faith,
A monstrous satanic God, a God of the blood's pantheism,
To come near satisfying the full extent of my imaginative frenzy
And never exhaust my desires to identify
With each and all and more-than-allness of your exploits!

Ah, torture me to cure me!
And this, my flesh—change it to that whoosh of air your slashing
                              cutlasses make
Before they fall on heads and shoulders!
Change my veins to the threads of clothes your knives cut through!
My imagination to the woman's body that you violate!
My intelligence to the deck you stand on when you kill!
And make my whole life—nervous, hysterical, absurd kit-and-
                              caboodle of it all—
Make it one huge organism with each act of piracy committed
One unit cell aware of it—and all of me whirling
Like one huge and undulating putrefaction—and let that be all!

In a sickening, immeasurable burst of speed,
The fever machine of my flooding visions
Now turns so that my consciousness in flight
Is scarcely more than a ring of smoke blown on the wind:

        Fifteen men on a Dead Man's Chest.
        Yo-ho-ho and a bottle of rum!

Hey there, hey there, ho-ho-ho, ha-ha-ha-ah-ah-ah . . .

Ah, the utter savagery of it all! Shit
On all life like ours that has nothing to do with it!
Here I am, an engineer, trained to use material energy, and aware
                              of all its forms,
Here I am stalled, where you're concerned, even when I'm walking;
Inert, even when I act; weak, even when I impose myself!
Static, broken, dissident coward of your Glory,

Da vossa grande dinâmica estridente, quente e sangrenta!

Arre! por não poder agir de acordo com o meu delírio!
Arre! por andar sempre agarrado às saias da civilização!
Por andar com a *douceur des mœurs* às costas, como um fardo de rendas!
Moços de esquina — todos nós o somos — do humanitarismo moderno!

Estupores de tísicos, de neurasténicos, de linfáticos,
Sem coragem para ser gente com violência e audácia,
Com a alma como uma galinha presa por uma perna!

Ah, os piratas! os piratas!
A ânsia do ilegal unido ao feroz,
A ânsia dos coisas absolutamente cruéis a abomináveis,
Que rói como um cio abstracto os nossos corpos franzinos,
Os nossos nervos femininos e delicados,
E põe grandes febres loucas nos nossos olhares vazios!

Obrigai-me a ajoelhar diante de vós!
Humilhai-me e batei-me!
Fazei de mim o vosso escravo e a vossa coisa!
E que o vosso desprezo por mim nunca me abandone,
Ó meus senhores! ó meus senhores!

Tomar sempre gloriosamente a parte submissa
Nos acontecimentos de sangue e nas sensualidades estiradas!
Desabai sobre mim, como grandes muros pesados,
Ó bárbaros do antigo mar!
Rasgai-me e feri-me!
De leste a oeste do meu corpo
Riscai de sangue a minha carne!

Beijai com cutelos de bordo e açoites e raiva
O meu alegre terror carnal de vos pertencer.
A minha ânsia mazoquista em me dar à vossa fúria,
Em ser objecto inerte e sentiente da vossa omnívora crueldade,
Dominadores, senhores, imperadores, corcéis!
Ah, torturai-me,

Your great, strident, hot and bloody dynamism!

Damn it! for being unable to act out my madness!
Damn it! for always traipsing around, tied to the apron strings
                    of civilization!
And going around burdened with my beautiful manners, like a load
                    of lace on my back!
Hangers-on—that we all are—of modern humanitarianism!

Consumptives, neurasthenics, lymphatics in our languors,
Lacking the courage to be bold and violent men,
Dragging our soul behind like a chicken's leg tied by a string!

Ah, the pirates! the pirates!
The itch to do something illegal and savage,
The itch to do absolutely cruel abominable things,
Like an abstract rut gnawing our fragile bodies,
Our delicate feminine nerves,
Till great mad fevers burn in our empty gazes!

Make me kneel before you!
Humiliate me and beat me!
Make me your slave and your object!
And let your scorn for me never abandon me,
O my masters, o my masters!

Let me always assume gloriously the submissive role
In bloody events and drawn-out sex bouts,
Fall on me like big heavy walls,
Oh barbarians of the ancient sea!
Tear me apart and maim me!
Going from east to west of my body,
Scratch bloody trails through my flesh!

Kiss with cutlass, boarding axe and frenzy
My joyous fleshly terror of belonging to you,
My masochistic itch to give in to your fury,
The sentient, inert object of your omnivorous cruelty—
Dominators, masters, emperors, corsairs!
Ah, torture me,

Rasgai-me e abri-me!
Desfeito em pedaços conscientes
Entornai-me sobre os conveses,
Espalhai-me nos mares, deixai-me
Nas praias ávidas das ilhas!

Cevai sobre mim todo o meu misticismo de vós!
Cinzelai a sangue a minh'alma
Cortai, riscai!
Ó tatuadores da minha imaginação corpórea!
Esfoladores amados da minha carnal submissão!
Submetei-me como quem mata um cão a pontapés!
Fazei de mim o poço para o vosso desprezo de domínio!

Fazei de mim as vossas vítimas todas!
Como Cristo sofreu por todos os homens, quero sofrer
Por todas as vossas vítimas às vossas mãos,
Às vossas mãos calosas, sagrentas e de dedos decepados
Nos assaltos bruscos de amuradas!

Fazei de mim qualquer cousa como se eu fosse
Arrastado — ó prazer, ó beijada dor! —
Arrastado à cauda de cavalos chicoteados por vós...
Mas isto no mar, isto no ma-a-a-ar, isto no MA-A-A-AR!
Eh-eh-eh-eh-eh! Eh-eh-eh-eh-eh-eh-eh!EH-EH-EH-EH-EH-EH-EH!
                                No MA-A-A-A-AR!

Yeh eh-eh-eh-eh-eh! Yeh-eh-eh-eh-eh-eh!Yeh-eh-eh-eh-eh-eh-eh-eh!
Grita tudo! tudo a gritar! ventos, vagas, barcos,
Marés, gáveas, piratas, a minha alma, o sangue, e o ar, e o ar!
Eh-eh-eh-eh! Yeh-eh-eh-eh-eh! Yeh-eh-eh-eh-eh-eh! Tudo canta a gritar!

FIFTEEN MEN ON THE DEAD MAN'S CHEST.
YO-HO-HO AND A BOTTLE OF RUM!

Eh-eh eh-eh -eh-eheh! Eh-eh-eh-eh-eheh-eh! Eh eh-eh eh-eh-eh-eh!
Eh-lahô-lahô-laHO-O-O-ôô-lahá-á-á — ààà!

AHÓ-Ó-Ó Ó Ó Ó-Ó Ó Ó Ó — yyy!
SCHOONER AHÓ-Ó-Ó-Ó-Ó-Ó-Ó-Ó-Ó-Ó — yyy!

Slash me, rip me open!
As I lie broken in small, conscious pieces
Spill me across decks,
Scatter me over seas, leave me
On the islands' greedy beaches!

Gratify on me all the mysticism I have claimed for you!
Chisel your way through my blood to my soul.
Cut and tear!
Oh tattooers of my corporeal imagination!
Flayer-lovers of my bodily submission!
Subdue me like a dog you kick to death!
Make me the sewer of your scorn of mastery!

Make me all your victims!
Like Christ who suffered for mankind, I'd suffer
For every victim of your hands—
Calloused, bloody hands with fingers split
By your violent boardings at the gunwales!

Make of me a blob that has been
Dragged—oh my delight, oh kiss of pain!—
Dragged at the tail of horses you have whipped . . .
But all this on the sea—on the se-eea, on the SE-EEEA!
Ho-ho-ho-ho! Ho-ho-ho-ho—on the S-EE-EEA!

Yah-yah-yah-yah! Yah-yah-yah-yah! Yah-yah-yah-yah-yah!
Everything screams! Everything is screaming! Winds, waves, ships!
Seas, topsails, pirates, my soul, blood, and the air, the air!
Ha-ha-ha——ha! Yah-yah-yah-yah! Yah-yah-yah-yah-yah-yah!
                              Everything screaming and singing!

FIFTEEN MEN ON A DEAD MAN'S CHEST.
YO-HO-HO AND A BOTTLE OF RUM!

Ha-ha-ha-ha-ha! Yah-yah-yah-yah! Yah-yah-yah-yah!
Ho-ho-ho-ho-ho! Ho-ho-ho-ho-ho! Hohohohohohoh!

AHO-O-O O O O O O-O O O O O—yyy! . .
SCHOONER AHO-O-O-O-O-O-O-O-O-O—yyy! . . .

Darby M'Graw-aw-aw-aw-aw-aw!
DARBY M'GRAW-AW AW-AW-AW-AW-AW!
FETCH A-A-AFT THE RU-U-U-U-U-UM, DARBY!

Eh-eh-eh-eh-eh-eh-eh-eh-eh-eh eh-eh-eh!
EH-EH-EH-EH-EH-EH-EH-EH-EH EH EH-EH-EH!
EH-EH-EH-EH-EH-EH-EH-EH-EH-EH-EH-EH!
EH-EH-EH-EH-EH-EH-EH-EH-EH-EH-EH!

EH-EH-EH-EH-EH-EH-EH-EH

Parte-se em mim qualquer coisa. O vermelho anoiteceu.
Senti demais para poder continuar a sentir.
Esgotou-se-me a alma, ficou só um eco dentro de mim.
Decresce sensìvelmente a velocidade do volante.
Tiram-me um pouco as mãos dos olhos os meus sonhos.
Dentro de mim há um só vácuo, um deserto, um mar nocturno.
E logo que sinto que há um mar nocturno dentro de mim,
Sabe dos longes dele, nasce do seu silêncio,
Outra vez, outra vez o vasto grito antiquíssimo.
De repente, com o um relâmpago de som, que não fez berulho mas
                                                          ternura,
Sùbitamente abrangendo todo o horizonte marítimo
Húmido e sombrio marulho humano nocturno,
Voz de sereia longínqua chorando, chamando,
Vem do fundo do Longe, do fundo do Mar, da alma dos Abismos,
E à tona dele, como algas, bóiam meus sonhos desfeitos...

Aho-ò-ò-ò-ò-ò-ò-ò-ò-ò-ò — yy...
Schooner ahò-ò-ò-ò-ò-ò-ò-ò-ò-ò-ò-ò — yy...

Ah, o orvalho sobre a minha excitação!
O frescor nocturno no meu oceano interior!
Eis tudo em mim de repente ante uma noite no mar
Cheia de enorme mistério humaníssimo das ondas nocturnas.
A lua sobe no horizonte
E a minha infância feliz acorda, como uma lágrima, em mim.
O meu passado ressurge, como se esse grito marítimo
Fosse um aroma, uma voz, o eco duma canção
Que fosse chamar ao meu passado
Por aquela felicidade que nunca mais tornarei a ter.

Darby M'Graw-aw-aw-aw-aw-aw!
DARBY M'GRAW-AW-AW-AW-AW-AW-AW!
FETCH AFFFT THE RU-U-U-U-UM, DARBY!

Ho-ho-ho-ho-ho-ho-ho-ho-ho-ho-ho-ho-ho!
HO-HO-HO-HO-HO-HO-HO-HO-HO-HO-HO-HO!
HO-HO-HO-HO-HO-HO-HO-HO-HO-HO-HO-HO!
HO-HO-HO-HO-HO-HO-HO-HO-HO-HO!

HO- HO- HO- HO- HO- HO- !

Something in me comes apart. A redness glows into dusk.
I've felt too much to go on feeling any more.
My soul is spent, an echo is all that's left inside me.
The flywheel slows down noticeably.
My dreams raise their hands a bit from over my eyes.
Inside I feel merely a vacuum, a desert, a nocturnal sea.
And as soon as I feel a nocturnal sea inside me
There rises up out of its distances, born of its silence,
Once more, once more, that vast, most ancient cry of all,
Suddenly as a light resounds with tenderness, not sound,
And instantly spreads all across the watery horizon,
The gloomy, humid surge of night-time humanity.
A distant siren voice comes wailing, calling out,
From depths of Distance, depths of Ocean, the center of Abysses,
While on the surface float like seaweed my dismembered dreams . . .

Aho-o-o-o-o-o-o-o-o-o-o—yy . . .
Schooner aho-o-o-o-o-o-o-o-o-o-o-o-o—yy . . . . .

Ah, this light dew that covers my excitement!
This night-freshness out of my internal sea!
There it is, suddenly before me, a sea night
Full of the enormous human mystery of night waves.
The moon rises on the horizon
And my happy childhood stirs, like a tear, inside me.
My past surges back and that seafaring cry
Becomes a fragrance, a voice, the echo of a song,
As if to recall my childhood
And evoke that happiness that I can never know again.

Era na velha casa sossegada ao pé do rio...
(As janelas do meu quarto, e as da casa-de-jantar também,
Davam, por sobre umas casas baixas, para o rio próximo,
Para o Tejo, este mesmo Tejo, mas noutro ponto, mais abaixo...
se eu agora chegass as mesmas janelas não chegava às mesmas Janelas.
Aquele tempo passou como o fumo dum vapor no mar alto...)

Uma inexplicável ternura,
Um remorso comovido e lacrimoso,
Por todas aquelas vítimas — principalmente as crianças —
Que sonhei fazendo ao sonhar-me pirata antigo,
Emoção comovida, porque elas foram minhas vítimas;
Terna e sauve, porque não o foram realmente;
Uma ternura confusa, como um vidro embaciado, azulada,
Canta velhas canções na minha pobre alma dolorida.

Ah, como pude eu pensar, sonhar aquelas coisas?
Que longe estou do que fui há uns momentos!
Histeria das sensações — ora estas, ora as opostas!
Na loura manhã que se ergue, como o meu ouvido só escolhe
As cousas de acordo com esta emoção — o marulho das águas,
O marulho leve das águas do rio de encontro ao cais...,
A vela passando perto do outro lado do rio,
Os montes longínquos, dum azul japonês,
As casas de Almada,
E o que há de suavidade e de infância na hora matutina!...

Uma gaivota que passa,
E a minha ternura é maior.

Mas todo este tempo não estive a reparar para nada.
Tudo isto foi uma impressão só da pele, com uma carícia
Todo este tempo não tirei os olhos do meu sonho longínquo,
Da minha casa ao pé do rio,
Da minha infância ao pé do rio,
Das janelas do meu quarto dando para o rio de noite,
E a paz do luar esparso nas águas!...

It was in the old, quiet house along the riverside . . .
(The windows of my room, and the dining room too,
Look out past low-lying houses, over the nearby river,
Over the Tagus, this very Tagus, but from somewhere else, farther
                                        down . . .
If I returned to the same windows now I would not find the same
                                        windows.
That time has gone like a steamer's smoke on the high seas . . .)

An inexplicable tenderness,
A sad, a touching regret,
For all those victims—especially the children—
I dreamed of, imagining myself an old pirate,
A touching feeling, because they were my victims;
Gentle, soft—since they really weren't;
A confused tenderness, like a blurry windowpane turning blue,
Sings sad old songs in my poor sad soul.

Ah, how could I have thought and dreamt of such things?
How removed I am now from what I was a few minutes ago!
The hysteria of one's sensations—now one thing, then just the
                                        opposite!
Now in this pale morning light my hearing picks out
Those things in tune with this new emotion—the splash of
                                        the waters,
The light lapping waters as the river touches the docks . . .
The sails passing near the river bank opposite,
The far-off hills in Japanese blue
Against the houses of Almada,
And all in gentle, newborn, in the early dawn hour! . . .

A sea gull passes.
My tenderness increases.

Yet all this time I noticed nothing around me.
It was all something I felt on my skin, like a caress.
All this time I didn't take my eyes off my distant dream,
My house at the riverside,
My childhood by the river,
With the windows of my room looking out at the river at night,
And the peaceful moonlight spread over the waters . . .

Minha velha tia, que me amava por causa do filho que perdeu . . . ,
Minha vilha tia costumava adormecer-me cantando-me
(Se bem que eu fosse já crescido demais para isso) . . .
Lembro-me e as lágrimas caem sobre o meu corção e lavam-o da vida.
E ergue-me uma leve brisa marítima dentro de mim.
As vezes ela cantava a «Nau Catrineta»:

> *Lá vai a Nau Catrineta*
> *Por sobre as águas do mar . . .*

E outras vezes, numa melodia muito saudosa e tão medieval,
Era a «Bela Infanta» . . . Relembro, e a pobre velha voz ergue-se
                                                    dentro de mim
E lembra-me que pouco me lembrei dela depois, e ela amava-me tanto!
Como fui ingrato para ela — e afinal que fiz eu da vida?
Era a «Bela Infanta» . . . Eu fechava os olhos, e ela cantava:

> *Estando a Bela Infanta*
> *No seu jardim assentada*

Eu abria um pouco os olhos e via a janela cheia de luar
E depois fechava os olhos outra vez, e em tudo isto era feliz.

> *Estando a Bela Infanta*
> *No seu jardim assentada,*
> *Seu pente de ouro na mão,*
> *Seus cabelos penteava*

O meu passado de infância, boneco que me partiram!

Não poder viajar pra o passado, para aquela casa e aquela afeição,
E ficar lá sempre, sempre criança e sempre contente!

Mas tudo isto foi o Passado, lanterna a uma esquina de rua velha.
Pensar isto faz frio, faz fome duma cousa que se não pode obter.
Dá-me não sei que remorso absurdo pensar nisto.
Oh turbilhão lento de sensações desencontradas!

My old aunt who loved me because of the son she'd lost . . .
My old aunt used to sing me to sleep
(Though I was already too grown-up for lullabies)—
I recall this, and tears well up in my heart and cleanse my life,
And a light sea breeze rises inside me.
Sometimes she'd sing of "The Good Ship Catrineta":

> *There goes the good ship Catrineta*
> *Over the sea and the waves.*

Or that song, so nostalgic and medieval,
About "The Fair Princess" . . . I recall it now, and the poor
                              woman's old voice stirs inside me,
Reminding me how little I've remembered since, and how much
                              she loved me!
And how ungrateful I was to her . . . and finally, what have I
                              done with my life?
"The Fair Princess" went . . . I'd close my eyes and she'd sing,

> *As the fair princess*
> *Sat in her garden*

I'd open my eyes a bit and see the window full of moonlight,
Then I'd shut my eyes again, so happy about it all.

> *As the fair princess*
> *Sat in her garden,*
> *Combing her tresses,*
> *Her comb was golden . . .*

Oh my childhood, a doll they broke for me!

I cannot go back to the past, that house and all that affection,
And stay there forever, forever a child and forever happy!

Well, it was all the Past, a lamp-post on an old streetcorner.
To think of it makes me cold, hungry for what I can't have.
To think of it makes me absurdly, indefinably bitter.
Oh slow whirlwind of feeling, flying off in every direction!

Vertigem ténue de confusas coisas na alma!
Fúrias partidas, ternuras como carrinhos de linha com que as
                                    crianças brincam,
Grandes desabamentos de imaginação sobre os olhos dos sentidos,
Lágrimas, lágrimas inúteis,
Leves brisas de contradição roçando pela face a alma...

Evoco, por um esforço voluntário, para sair desta emoção,
Evoco, com um esforço desesperado, seco, nulo,
A canção do Grande Pirata, quando estava a morrer;

> *Fifteen men on the Dead Man's Chest.*
> *Yo-ho-ho and a bottle of rum!*

Mas a canção é uma linha recta mal traçada dentro de mim...

Esforço-me e consigo chamar outra vez ante os meus olhos na alma,
Outra vez, mas através duma imaginação quase literária,
A fúria da pirataria, da chacina, o apetite, quase do paladar, do saque,
Da chacina inútil de mulheres e de crianças,
Da tortura fútil, e só para nos distrairmos, dos passageiros pobres
E a sensualidade de escangalhar e partir as coisas mais queridas
                                    dos outros,
Mas sonho isto tudo com um medo de qualquer coisa a respirar-me
                                    sobre a nuca.

Lembro-me de que seria interessante
Enforcar os filhos à vista das mães
(Mas sinto-me sem querer as mães deles),
Enterrar vivas nas ilhas desertas as crianças de quatro anos
Levando os pais em barcos até lá para verem
(Mas estremeço, lembrando-me dum filho que não tenho e está
                                    dormindo tranquilo em casa).

Aguilhoo uma ânsia fria dos crimes marítimos,
Duma inquisição sem a desculpa da Fé,
Crimes nem sequer com razão de ser de maldade e de fúria,

Tenuous, vertiginous confusions of the soul!
Spent rages, affections like spools of thread children play with,
The imagination collapsing in full gaze of all one's senses,
Tears, useless tears,
Light contrary winds grazing the soul . . .

To escape such feelings, I deliberately evoke,
By a desperate, dry, and empty effort of the will, I evoke
The song of the Great Pirate, about to die.

> *Fifteen men on a Dead Man's Chest.*
> *Yo-ho-ho and a bottle of rum!*

But the song fades like a poorly traced straight line inside me . . .

I force myself again, and succeed in calling up before my
                                                    gazing soul
Again, though through the medium of a semi-literary imagination,
The pirates' fury, love of slaughter, appetite, and almost physical
                                                    taste for plunder,
The pointless slaughter of women and of children,
The useless torture of the poor passengers, only to amuse
                                                    themselves,
And the lust to smash those things most cherished by the others,
But as I dream all this I'm afraid of something breathing down
                                                    my neck.

I remember how interesting it would be
To hang children before their mothers' eyes
(Though involuntarily feeling I'm the children's mothers),
To bury four-year-olds on desert islands,
Rowing their fathers up to see it done
(Though it makes me shudder, recalling a child I never had,
                                                    peacefully asleep at home.)

I incite a cold passion for crimes at sea,
An Inquisition with no excuse of Faith,
Crimes with no motive, not even malice and anger,

Feitos a frio, nem sequer para ferir, nem sequer para fazer mal,
Nem sequer para nos divertirmos, mas apenas para passar o tempo,
como quem faz paciências a uma mesa de jantar de província com
    a toalha atirada pra o outro lado da mesa depois de jantar,
Só pelo suave gosto de cometer crimes abomináveis e não os achar
                          grande coisa,
De ver sofrer até ao ponto da loucura e da morte-pela-dor mas
                        nunca deixar chegar lá...
Mas a minha imaginação recusa-se a acompanhar-me.
Um calafrio arrepia-me.
E de repente, mais de repente do que da outra vez, de mais longe,
                        de mais fundo,
De repente — oh pavor por todas as minhas veias! —,
Oh frio repentino da porta para o Mistério que se abriu dentro de
                    mim e deixou entrar uma corrente de ar!
Lembro-me de Deus, do Transcendental da vida, e de repente
A velha voz do marinheiro inglês Jim Barns com quem eu falava,
Tornada voz das ternuras misteriosas dentro de mim, das pequenas
            coisas de regaço de mãe e de fita de cabelo de irmã,
Mas estupendamente vinda de além da aparência das coisas,
A Voz surda e remota tornada A Voz Absoluta, a Voz Sem Boca,
Vinda de sobre e de dentro do solidão nocturna dos mares,
Chama por mim, chama por mim, chama por mim...

Vem surdamente, como se fosse suprimida e se ouvisse,
Longìnquamente, como se estivesse soando noutro lugar e aqui não
                  se pudesse ouvir,
Como um soluço abafado, uma luz que se apaga, um hálito silencioso,
De nenhum lado do espaço, de nenhum local no tempo,
O grito eterno e nocturno, o sopro fundo e confuso:

Ahô-ô-ô-ô-ô-ô-ô-ô-ô-ô-ô — yyy......
Ahô-ô-ô-ô-ô-ô-ô-ô-ô-ô-ô-ô-ô-ô-ô — — yy......
Schooner ah-ô-ô-ô-ô-ô-ô-ô-ô-ô-ô-ô-ô-ô-ô-ô — — yy.....

Tremo com frio da alma repassando-me o corpo
E abro de reprente o olhos, que não tinha fechado.
Ah, que alegria a de sair dos sonhos de vez!

Done in cold blood, not even to hurt or do wrong,
Not for a joke, but just to kill time,
Like someone playing solitaire at the dinner table in the country,
     the tablecloth pushed to one side after dinner,
Just for the fun of committing abominable crimes and not thinking
     twice about it,
Just to see someone suffer, go crazy and dying of pain, yet never
     letting it come to that point . . .
But my imagination refuses to follow me.
A chill makes my hair stand on end,
And suddenly (more suddenly than before, more distant and more
     profound in suddenness)
—oh the fright that freezes my veins!—all of a sudden
That sudden cold as the door to the Mystery opens inside me
     and lets in a draught!
I remember God, the Transcendent-in-life, and suddenly
The old voice of the British sailor Jim Barnes with whom I used
     to talk,
Becomes now inside me the voice of mysterious endearments,
     with all those little details of being in my
     mother's lap and my sister's hair-ribbon,
But now stupendously borne from the other side of the appearance
     of things,
The deafening, far-off Voice become the Absolute Voice, the
     Mouthless Voice,
Borne from the surface and depths of the sea's nocturnal Solitude,
Calling me, calling me, calling me . . .

It comes through muffled, as though stifled but still audible,
From far far away, as though sounding elsewhere and not hearable,
Like a smothered cry, a doused light, a silenced breath.
From no point in space, from no place in time,
The everlasting night cry, the deep, confusing exhalation:

   Aho-o-o-o-o-o-o-o-oo---yyy . . . . .
   Aho-o-o-o-o-o-o-o-o-o-o---yyy . . . . .
   Schooner aho-o-o-o-o-o-o-o-o-o-o-oo---yy . . . . .

A cold shiver passes through my body from the depths of my soul
And I quickly open my eyes that I hadn't closed.
Ah, what joy coming out of my dreams at once!

Eis outra vez o mundo real, tão bondoso para os nervos!
Ei-lo a esta hora matutina em que entram os paquetes que chegam ced

Já não me importa o paquete que entrava. Ainda está longe.
Só o que está perto agora me lava a alma.
A minha imaginação higiénica, forte, prática,
Preocupa-se agora apenas com as coisas modernas e úteis,
Com os navios de carga, com os paquetes e os passageiros,
Com as fortes coisas imediatas, modernas, comerciais, verdadeiras.
Abranda o seu giro dentro de mim o volante.

Maravilhosa vida marítima moderna,
Todo limpeza, máquinas e saúde!
Tudo tão bem arranjado, tão espontâneamente adjustado,
Todas as peças das máquinas, todos os navios pelos mares,
Todos os elementos da actividade comercial de exportação e importaç
Tão maravilhosamente combinando-se
Que corre tudo como se fosse por leis naturais,
Nenhuma coisa esbarrando com outra!

Nada perdeu a poesia. E agora há a mais as máquinas
Com a sua poesia também, e todo o novo género de vida
Comercial, mundana, intelectual, sentimental,
Que a era das máquinas veio trazer para as almas.
As viagens agora são tão belas como eram dantes
E um navio será sempre belo, só porque é um navio.
Viajar ainda é viajar e o longe está sempre onde esteve —
Em parte nenhuma, graças a Deus!

Os portos cheios de vapores de muitas espécies!
Pequenos, grandes, de várias cores, com várias disposições de vigias,
De tão deliciosamente tantas companhias de navegação!
Vapores nos portos, tão individuais na separação destacada dos
                                                    ancoramentos!

Here's the real world again, so good for the nerves!
Here's the early morning with its newly-arrived ship entering
                    the port.

Which ship has arrived doesn't matter a bit. It's still far off.
Only what's close up now warms the heart.
Now it's my imagination, strong, practical, hygienic,
That busies itself only with modern and useful things,
With freighters, steamships and passengers,
With powerful, immediate, modern, commercial, down-to-earth
                    things.
The flywheel inside me slows down.

Wonderful modern maritime life,
Everything so sanitary, mechanized, healthy!
Everything so well-regulated, so spontaneously adjusted,
All the cogs and wheels, all the ships at sea,
All facets of mercantile enterprise, export and import,
So marvelously managed
That everything runs as if by natural law,
Nothing jarring or out of place!

Poetry hasn't lost out a bit. Moreover, we now have the machine
With its own poetry as well, and a totally new way of life,
Businesslike, worldly, intellectual, sentimental,
Which the machine age has endowed our souls with.
Voyages are now as beautiful as they ever were,
And a ship will always be beautiful, simply because it's a ship.
A sea voyage is still a sea voyage and distance exists where it
                    always did—
Nowhere, thank God!

Seaports full of steamships of every conceivable type!
Large and small, and all painted differently, each with its
                    distinct schedule of watches for its crew,
Each one exquisitely following the choice of one of so many
                    companies!
Each steamer in port so unique in its well-marked mooring!

Tão prazenteiro o seu garbo quieto de cousas comerciais que andam
no mar,
No velho mar sempre o homérico, ó Ulisses!

O olhar humanitário dos faróis na distância da noite,
Ou o súbito farol próximo na noite muito escura
(«Que perto da terra que estávamos passando!» E o som da água
canta-nos ao ouvido)!...

Tudo isto hoje é como sempre foi, mas há o comércio;
E o destino comercial dos grandes vapores
Envaidece-me da minha época!
A mistura de gente a bordo dos navios de passageiros
Dá-me o orgulho moderno de viver numa época onde é tão fácil
Misturarem-se as raças, transporem-se os espaços, ver com facilidade
todas as coisas,
E gozar a vida realizando um grande número de sonhos.

Limpos, regulares, modernos como um escritório com *guichets* em
redes de arame amarelo,
Meus sentimentos agora, naturais e comedidos como *gentlemen,*
São práticos, longe de desvairamentos, enchem de ar marítimo os puli
Como gente perfeitamente consciente de como é higiénico respirar
o ar do mar.

O dia é perfeitamente já de horas de trabalho.
Começa tudo a movimentar-se, a regularizar-se.
Com um grande prazer natural e directo percorro a alma
Todas as operações comerciais necessárias a um embarque de mercad
A minha época é o carimbo que levam todas as facturas,
E sinto que todas as cartas de todos os escritórios
Deviam ser endereçadas a mim.

Um conhecimento de bordo tem tanta individualidade,
E uma assinatura de comandante de navio é tão bela e moderna!
Rigor comercial do princípio e do fim das cartas:
Dear Sirs — Messieurs — Amigos e Srs.,

So festive in the quiet elegance of its commercial traffic on
        the seaways,
Over the always ancient Homeric seaways, oh Ulysses!

The humanitarian glance of the lighthouses far out at night
Or the sudden glare of the lighthouse beam nearby on a dark
        thick night
("How close we must now be to land!" And the water sings in
        our ears)! . . .

All this today is what's always been, except that there's trade,
And the commercial purpose of the great ships
Makes me boast of this age I live in!
The variety of people aboard passenger ships
Fills me with the modern pride of living in an age when it's so easy
For races to come together, cover distances, and see all the new
        things so easily,
Thus making real and enjoying in one's lifetime a great many
        things only dreamt of before!

Clean, adjusted, and modern as an office of counters enclosed
        in yellow wire netting,
My feelings now are ordinary and respectable as *gentlemen,*
Being practical and wholly undistracted, they fill the lungs
        with sea air,
Like people perfectly aware of how salubrious it is to inhale sea air.

Now the day starts perfectly as a working day.
It all gets underway, everything falling into place.
With great pleasure, natural and straightforward, I recite by heart
All the commercial operations needed to get a shipment of goods
        on its way.
My age is the rubber stamp appearing on all invoices
And I feel that all letters in all offices
Must be addressed to me.

A knowledge of shipping is so distinctive,
And a ship captain's signature is so beautiful and modern!
The strict commercial style of beginning and ending a letter:
Dear Sirs—Messieurs—Amigos e Srs.,

Yours faithfully — . . . nos salutations empressées . . .
Tudo isto não é só humano e limpo, mas também belo,
E tem ao fim um destino marítimo, um vapor onde embarquem
As mercadorias de que as cartas e as facturas tratam.

Complexidade da vida! As facturas são feitas por gente
Que tem amores, ódios, paixões políticas, às vezes crimes —
E são tão bem escritas, tão alinhadas, tão independentes de tudo isso!
Há quem olhe para uma factura e não sinta isto.
Com certeza que tu, Cesário Verde, o sentias.
Eu é até às lágrimas que o sinto humaníssimamente.
Venham dizer-me que não há poesia no comércio, nos escritórios!
Ora, ela entra por todos poros . . . Neste ar marítimo respiro-a,
Por tudo isto vem a propósito dos vapores, da navegação moderna,
Porque as facturas e as cartas comerciais são o princípio da história
E os navios que levam as mercadorias pelo mar eterno são o fim.

Ah, e as viagens, as viagens de recreio, e as outras
As viagens por mar, onde todos somos companheiros dos outros
Duma maneira especial, como se um mistério marítimo
Nos aproximasse as almas e nos tornasse um momento
Patriotas transitóres duma mesma pátria incerta,
Eternamente deslocando-se sobre a imensidade das águas!
Grandes hotéis do Infinito, oh transatlânticos meus!
Com o cosmopolitismo perfeito e total de nunca pararem num ponto
E conterem todas as espécies de trajes, de caras, de raças!

As viagens, os viajantes — tantas espécies deles!
Tanta nacionalidade sobre o mundo! tanta profissão! tanta gente!
Tanto destino diverso que se pode dar à vida,
À vida, afinal, no fundo sempre, sempre a mesma!
Tantas caras curiosas! Todas as caras são curiosas
E nada traz tanta religiosidade como olhar muito para gente.
A fraternidade afinal não é uma ideia revolucionária.

Your faithfully— . . . nos salutations empressées . . .
It's all not only human and tidy but also beautiful,
And finally it's all got a maritime purpose—the vessel with freight
Being shipped is what the letters and invoices are about.

Life's complexity! Invoices are made out by men
Who love and hate, have political passions, sometimes commit
crimes—
And their invoices are so well written, so perfectly aligned, so
independent of all that!—
There are those who can look at an invoice and not feel this at all.
Surely you, Cesário Verde, you once felt this.
As for me, I feel it so personally I can almost weep.
Don't tell me there's no poetry in business, in offices!
Why, it seeps through every pore . . .I breathe it in the sea air
Because it's all got to do with ships and modern navigation,
Because invoices and commercial letters are the beginnings of
history,
And ships carrying goods on the everlasting sea are its end.

And, ah, the voyages, the holiday cruises, and the rest,
The sea voyages where we all get to be fellow passengers
In a special way, as though some mystery of sea custom
Had touched our hearts and momentarily changed us
Into travelling compatriots of some indeterminate fatherland,
Forever changing location on the vast ocean!
Grand Hotels of the Infinite, oh my transatlantic liners!
With the totally perfect cosmopolitanism of never stopping at
any point
And encompassing every type of costume, countenance, and race!

Voyages and voyagers—and so many different types of them!
So many nationalities on earth, so many professions, so many
people!
So many different directions to steer one's life,
And life itself, in the end and at heart, always the same!
So many strange faces! All faces are strange
And nothing gives one the sense of what's holy so much as
watching people constantly.
Brotherhood isn't finally a revolutionary idea,

É uma coisa que a gente aprende pela vida fora, onde tem que tolerar tu
E passa a achar graça ao que tem que tolerar,
E acaba quase a chorar de ternura sobre o que tolerou!

Ah, tudo isto é belo, tudo isto é humano e anda ligado
Aos sentimentos humanos, tão conviventes e burgueses.
Tão complicadamente simples, tão metafìsicamente tristes!
A vida flutuante, diversa, acaba por nos educar no humano.
Pobre gente! pobre gente toda a gente!

Despeço-me desta hora no corpo deste outro navio
Que vai agora saindo. É um *tramp-steamer* inglês,
Muito sujo, como se fosse um navio francês,
Com um ar simpático de proletário dos mares,
E sem dúvida anunciado ontem na última página das gazetas.

Enternece-me o pobre vapor, tão humilde vai ele e tão natural.
Parece ter um certo escrúpulo não sei em quê, ser pessoa honesta,
Cumpridora duma qualquer espécie de deveres.
Lá vai ele deixando o lugar defronte do cais onde estou.
Lá vai ele tranquilamente, passando por onde as naus estiveram
Outrora, outrora...
Para Cardiff? Para Liverpool? Para Londres? Não tem importância.
Ele faz o seu dever. Assim façamos nós o nosso. Bela vida!
Boa viagem! Boa viagem!
Boa viagem, meu pobre amigo casual, que me fizeste o favor
De levar contigo a febre e a tristeza dos meus sonhos,
E restituir-me à vida para olhar para ti e te ver passar.
Boa viagem! Boa viagem! A vida é isto...

Que aprumo tão natural, tão inevitàvelmente matutino
Na tua saída do porto de Lisboa, hoje!
Tenho-te uma afeição curiosa e grata por isso...

It's something you learn by living your life, when you've got
                            to tolerate everything,
And where you begin finding pleasant what you've got to tolerate,
And you end up nearly weeping with tenderness over the things
                            you tolerate!

Ah, and all this is beautiful, all this is human and firmly tied up
To the life of feelings—so human, so sociable, so bourgeois,
So complexly simple, so metaphysically sad!
Drifting, diverse, life ends by teaching us to be human.
Poor people! Poor people, all of us, everywhere!

I take leave of this moment in the shape of this other ship
Setting out now. It's an English *tramp steamer,*
Filthy enough to be French,
With the homely look of a seafaring proletarian,
And listed no doubt on the last page of yesterday's shipping-news.

The poor ship touches me, it moves so humbly and naturally.
There's a certain scrupulousness about it—in what way I can't
                           say—like an honest person
Going about doing whatever he has to do.
Now it's moving away from the dock in front of me, from the spot
                           where I'm standing.
There it goes quietly by where caravels used to go by
Long ago, long long ago . . .
Headed for Cardiff? Liverpool? London? It doesn't matter where.
It's doing its job. Like us doing ours. Life is so beautiful!
Bon voyage! Bon voyage!
Bon voyage, poor passing acquaintance, you did me the favor
Of sharing with you the fever and fret of my thoughts,
And bringing me back to life so I could think of you and watch
                           you go by.
Bon voyage! Bon voyage! That's what life is . . .

Your poise is so natural, so inevitably matutinal,
Leaving Lisbon harbor today,
You fill me with a curious familiar affection for . . .

Por isso quê? Sei lá o que é!... Vai... Passa...
Com um ligeiro estremecimento,
(T-t--t---t----t-----t...)
O volante dentro de mim pára.

Passa, lento vapor, passo e não fiques...
Passa de mim, passa da minha vista,
Vai-te de dentro do meu coração,
Perde-te no Longe, no Longe, bruma de Deus,
Perde-te, segue o teu destino e deixa-me...
Eu quem sou para que chore e interrogue?
Eu quem sou para que te fale e te ame?
Eu quem sou para que me perturbe ver-te?
Larga do cais, cresce o sol, ergue-se ouro,
Luzem os telhados dos edifícios do cais,
Todo o lado de cá da cidade brilha...
Parte, deixa-me, torna-te
Primeiro o navio a meio do rio, destacado e nítido,
Depois o navio a caminho da barra, pequeno e preto.
Depois ponto vago no horizonte (ó minha angústia!),
Ponto cada vez mais vago no horizonte...,
Nada depois, e só eu e a minha tristeza,
E a grande cidade agora cheia de sol
E a hora real e nua como um cais já sem navios,
E o giro lento do guindaste que, como um compasso que gira,
Traça um semicírculo de não sei que emoção
No silêncio comovido da minh'alma...

For what? Well, I know what's out there! . . . But go ahead . . .
                              pass by . . .
With a slight shudder
(T-t--t---t----t . . .)
The flywheel inside me stops.

Slow ship, pass by, pass away and don't stop . ..
Leave me, pass way out of sight,
Take yourself out of my heart,
Vanish in the Distance, the farthest Distance, the Mist of God,
Disappear, follow your destiny, leave me behind . . .
Who am I to weep and ask questions?
Who am I to speak to you and love you?
Who am I to be upset by the sight of you?
It leaves the dock, the sun rises, turns golden,
The roofs of buildings along the dock begin to glow,
This whole side of the city is sparkling . . .
Goodbye now, leave me—first be
The ship in midriver, standing there bright and clear,
Then, the ship passing the sandbar, small and black,
Then, a vague speck on the horizon (oh my dread!),
A speck growing vaguer and vaguer on the horizon . . .
Then, nothing at all—only me and my sorrow,
And now a great city full of sunlight,
And this moment, real and bare as a deserted dock,
And the slow-moving crane that turns like a compass
Tracing a semi-circular course of God knows what emotion
In the compassionate stillness of my heart . . .

4

Fernando Pessoa

Leve, breve, suave

Leve, breve, suave,
Um canto de ave
Sobe no ar com que principia
O dia.
Escuto, e passou. . .
Parece que foi só porque escutei
Que parou.

Nunca, nunca, em nada,
Raie a madrugada,
Ou'splenda o dia, ou doire no declive,
Tive
Prazer a durar
Mais do que o nada, a perda, antes de eu o ir
Gozar.

Ela canta, pobre ceifeira

Ela canta, pobre ceifeira,
Julgando-se feliz talvez;
Canta, e ceifa, e sua voz, cheia
De alegre e anónima viuvez,

Ondula como um canto de ave
No ar limpo como um limiar,
E há curvas no enredo suave
Do som que ela tem a cantar.

Ouvi-la alegra e entristece,
Na sua voz há o campo e a lida,
E canto como se tivesse
Mais razões p'ra cantar que a vida.

from *Uncollected Poems*

Lightly, quickly, soft

Lightly, quickly, soft,
A bird song
Climbs the sky as day
Begins.
I listen—it is gone.
It seemed to stop only because
I was listening.

Never, never in anything—
At dawn, in splendid daylight,
Or in the golden sunset—
Have I found
Any pleasure that would last
Beyond the nothingness, the loss, before coming
To enjoy it.

She is singing, poor reaper

She is singing, poor reaper,
Thinking she's happy perhaps;
Singing and reaping, and full
Of a widow's anonymous gladness.

Rising and falling like birdsong
In air as clean as a threshold,
Her undulant voice bears away
The lissome thread of her song.

Cheered but saddened, I listen.
All fields, all toil fill her voice
As if she were given more reason
To sing than life itself can give.

Ah, canta, canta sem razão!
O que em mim sente 'sta pensando.
Derrama no meu coração
A tua incerta voz ondeando!

Ah, poder ser tu, sendo eu!
Ter a tua alegre inconsciência,
E a consciência disso! Ó céu!
Ó campo! Ó canção! A ciência

Pesa tanto e a vida é tão breve!
Entrai por mim dentro! Tornai
Minha alma a vossa sombra leve!
Depois, levando-me, passai!

Gato que brincas na rua

Gato que brincas na rua
Como se fosse na cama,
Invejo a sorte que é tua.
Porque nem sorte se chama.

Bom servo das leis fatais
Que regem pedras e gentes,
Que tens instintos gerais
E sentes só o que sentes.

És feliz porque és assim,
Todo o nada que és é teu.
Eu vejo-me e estou sem mim,
Conheço-me e não sou eu.

Sing, sing, for no reason at all!
All feeling in me turns to thought.
Pour, pour into my soul
Your round voice, wavering.

Oh, to be you, yet myself,
Full of your glad unawareness
And yet still aware! O sky!
O fields! And that song! Learning

Comes slow and life is so brief!
Come through me, all of you—make me
The weightless shadow behind you,
Then gather me up and fly off!

Cat, you tumble down the street

Cat, you tumble down the street
As if it were your bed.
I think such luck's a treat,
Like feeding without being fed.

You're just a pawn in the hands
Of fate, as stones are, and people!
You follow your instinct and glands;
What you feel you feel—it's simple.

Because you're like that you're happy;
You're all the nothing you see.
I look at myself—it's not me.
I know myself—I'm not I.

Tenho tanto sentimento

Tenho tanto sentimento
Que é frequente persuadir-me
De que sou sentimental,
Mas reconheço, ao medir-me,
Que tudo isso é pensamento,
Que não senti afinal.

Temos, todos que vivemos,
Uma vida que é vivida
E outra vida que é pensada,
E a única vida que temos
É essa que é dividida
Entre a verdadeira e a errada.

Qual porém é verdadeira
E qual errada, ninguém
Nos saberá explicar;
E vivemos de maneira
Que a vida que a gente tem
É a que tem que pensar.

Durmo. Se sonho, ao despertar não sei

Durmo. Se sonho, ao despertar não sei
Que coisas eu sonhei.
Durmo. Se durmo sem sonhar, desperto
Para um espaço aberto
Que não conheço, pois que despertei
Para o que inda não sei.
Melhor é nem sonhar nem não sonhar
E nunca despertar.

I'm so full of feeling

I'm so full of feeling
I can easily believe
I must be sentimental.
But when I mull this over,
I see it's all in thought,
I felt nothing whatever.

All of us alive spend
One life in living it,
Another, thinking it.
And the only life we have
Is split between
The true one and the false.

But which is true
And which is false
Nobody can explain.
And as we go on living,
The life we spend's the one
That's doomed to thinking.

I sleep. If I dream, I do not know on waking

I sleep. If I dream, I do not know on waking
What it was I dreamt.
I sleep. If I do not dream, I waken
In an open space
I do not recognize, because I woke
To what I yet must come to know.
What's best is neither dreaming nor not dreaming,
But never waking.

Autopsicografia

O poeta é um fingidor.
Finge tão completamente
Que chega a fingir que é dor
A dor que deveras sente.

E os que lêem o que escreve,
Na dor lida sentem bem,
Não as duas que ele teve,
Mas só a que eles não têm.

E assim nas calhas de roda
Gira, a entreter a razão
Esse comboio de corda
Que se chama coração.

Isto

Dizem que finjo ou minto
Tudo que escrevo. Não.
Eu simplesmente sinto
Com a imaginação.
Não uso o coração.

Tudo o que sonho ou passo,
O que me falha ou finda,
É como que um terraço
Sobre outra coisa ainda.
Essa coisa é que é linda.

Por isso escrevo em meio
Do que não está ao pé,
Livre do meu enleio,
Sério do que não é.
Sentir? Sinto quem lê!

Autopsychography

The poet is a faker. He
Fakes it so completely,
He even fakes he's suffering
The pain he's really feeling.

And those of us who read his writing
Fully feel while reading
Not that pain of his that's double,
But one completely fictional.

So on its tracks goes round and round,
To entertain the reason,
That wound-up little train
We call the heart of man.

This

They say I fake or lie
In everything I write.
No, it's simply that
With me imagination
Feels—I don't use
The heart.

All I dream or go through,
All I fail or lose out
On, is like a terrace
Facing something else
Again. And that's the lovely
Thing.

It's why I write
Steeped in things not readily
At hand—free of emotions,
Serious about what isn't.
Feelings? That's the reader's
Lot.

Tomámos a Vila Depois dum Intenso Bombardamento

A criança loura
Jaz no meio da rua.
Tem as tripas de fora
E por uma corda sua
Um comboio que ignora.

A cara está um feixe
De sangue e de nada.
Luz um pequeno peixe
— Dos que bóiam nas banheiras —
À beira da estrada.

Cai sobre a estrada o escuro.
Longe, ainda uma luz doura
A criação do futuro...

E o da criança loura?

Sou um evadido

Sou um evadido.
Logo que nasci
Fecharam-me em mim,
Ah, mas eu fugi.

Se a gente se cansa
Do mesmo lugar,
Do mesmo ser
Por que não se cansar?

Minha alma procura-me
Mas eu ando a monte,
Oxalá que ela
Nunca me encontre.

We Took the Town After a Heavy Bombing

The little blond boy
Lies in the street.
His guts hang out
And a toy train loose
Loose on a string, forgotten.

His face is a mash
Of ooze and nothing.
A celluloid fish
Children float in a tub
Glints on the curb.

Darkness covers the street.
Far off a light still casts its glow
On all tomorrow promises . . .

For the little blond boy?

I'm a runaway

I'm a runaway.
When I was born
They shut me up
Inside myself.
Ah, but I ran away.

If people get sick
Of living in
The same old place,
Why not of living
In the same old skin?

My soul is on
The lookout for me,
But I lie low.
Will it ever find me?
Never, I hope!

Ser um é cadeia,
Ser eu é não ser.
Viverei fugindo
Mas vivo a valer.

Being myself only
Means being pinned down
And no one at all.
I'll live on the run,
And really live!

English Poems, from *35 Sonnets* (1918)

IV

I could not think of thee as pieced rot,
Yet such thou wert, for thou hadst been long dead;
Yet thou liv'dst entire in my seeing thought
And what thou wert in me had never fled.
Nay, I had fixed the moments of thy beauty—
Thy ebbing smile, thy kiss's readiness,
And memory had taught my heart the duty
To know thee ever at that deathlessness.
But when I came where thou wert laid, and saw
The natural flowers ignoring thee sans blame,
And the encroaching grass, with casual flaw,
Framing the stone to age where was thy name,
      I knew not how to feel, nor what to be
      Towards thy fate's material secrecy.

VI

As a bad orator, badly o'er-book-skilled,
Doth overflow his purpose with made heat,
And, like a clock, winds with withoutness willed
What should have been an inner instinct's feat;
Or as a prose-wit, harshly poet turned,
Lacking the subtler music in his measure,
With useless care labours but to be spurned,
Courting in alien speech the Muse's pleasure;
I study how to love or how to hate,
Estranged by consciousness from sentiment,
With a thought feeling forced to be sedate
Even when the feeling's nature is violent;
      As who would learn to swim without the river,
      When nearest to the trick, as far as ever.

XII

As the lone, frighted user of a night-road
Suddenly turns round, nothing to detect,
Yet on his fear's sense keepeth still the load
Of that brink-nothing he doth but suspect;
And the cold terror moves to him more near
Of something that from nothing casts a spell,
That, when he moves, to fright more is not there,
And's only visible when invisible:
So I upon the world turn round in thought,
And nothing viewing do no courage take,
But my more terror, from no seen cause got,
To that felt corporate emptiness forsake,
      And draw my sense of mystery's horror from
      Seeing no mystery's mystery alone.

XIV

We are born at sunset and we die ere morn,
And the whole darkness of the world we know,
How can we guess its truth, to darkness born,
The obscure consequence of absent glow?
Only the starts to teach us light. We grasp
Their scattered smallnesses with thoughts that stray,
And, though their eyes look through night's complete mask,
Yet they speak not the features of the day.
Why should these small denials of the whole
More than the black whole the pleased eyes attract?
Why what it calls "worth" does the captive soul
Add to the small and from the large detract?
      So, out of light's love wishing it night's stretch,
      A nightly thought of day we darkly reach.

XV

Like a bad suitor desperate and trembling
From the mixed sense of being not loved and loving,
Who with feared longing half would know, dissembling
With what he'd wish proved what he fears soon proving,
I look with inner eyes afraid to look,
Yet perplexed into looking, at the worth
This verse may have and wonder, of my book,
To what thoughts shall't in alien hearts give birth.
But, as he who doth love, and, loving, hopes,
Yet, hoping, fears, fears to put proof to proof,
And in his mind for possible proofs gropes,
Delaying the true proof, lest the real thing scoff,
       I daily live, i'th'fame I dream to see,
      But by my thought of others' thought of me.

XVII

My love, and not I, is the egoist.
My love for thee loves itself more than thee;
Ay, more than me, in whom it doth exist,
And makes me live that it may feed on me.
In the country of bridges the bridge is
More real than the shores it doth unsever;
So in our world, all of Relation, this
Is true—that truer is Love than either lover.
This thought therefore comes lightly to Doubt's door—
If we, seeing substance of this world, are not
Mere Intervals, God's Absence and no more,
Hollows in real Consciousness and Thought.
      And if 'tis possible to Thought to bear this, fruit,
      Why should it not be possible to Truth?

XX

When in the widening circle of rebirth
To a new flesh my travelled soul shall come,
And try again the unremembered earth
With the old sadness for the immortal home,
Shall I revisit these same differing fields
And cull the old new flowers with the same sense,
That some small breath of foiled remembrance yields,
Of more age than my days in this pretence?
Shall I again regret strange faces lost
Of which the present memory is forgot
And but in unseen bulks of vagueness tossed
Out of the closed sea and black night of Thought?
      Were thy face one, what sweetness will't not be,
      Though by blind feeling, to remember thee!

XXVI

The world is woven all of dream and error
And but one sureness in our truth may lie—
That when whe hold to aught our thinking's mirror
We know it not by knowing it thereby.
For but one side of things the mirror shows,
And knows it colded from its solidness.
A double lie its truth is; what it shows
By true show's false and nowhere by true place.
Thought clouds our life's day-sense with strangeness, yet
Never from strangeness more than that it's strange
Doth buy our perplexed thinking, for we get
But the words' sense from words—knowledge, truth, change.
      We know the world is false, not what is true.
      Yet we think on, knowing, we ne'er shall know.

XXVIII

The edge of the green wave whitely doth hiss
Upon the wetted sand. I look, yet dream.
Surely reality cannot be this!
Somehow, somewhere this surely doth but seem!
The sky, the sea, this great extent disclosed
Of outward joy, this bulk of life we feel,
Is not something, but something interposed.
Only what in this is not this is real.
If this be to have sense, if to be awake
Be but to see this bright, great sleep of things,
For the rarer potion mine own dreams I'll take
And for truth commune with imaginings,
       Holding a dream too bitter, a too fair curse,
       This common sleep of men, the universe.

XXXV

Good. I have done. My heart weighs. I am sad.
The outer day, void statue of lit blue,
Is altogether outward, other glad
At mere being not-I (so my aches construe).
I, that have failed in everything, bewail
Nothing this hour but that I have bewailed,
For in the general fate what is't to fail?
Why, fate being past for Fate, 'tis but to have failed.
Whatever hap or stop, what matters it,
Sith to the mattering our will bringeth nought?
With the higher trifling let us world our wit,
Conscious that, if we do't, that was the lot
       The regular stars bound us to, when they stood
       Godfathers to our birth and to our blood.

From "The Genesis of My Heteronyms"

... I put into Caeiro all my power of dramatic depersonalization, into Ricardo Reis all my intellectual discipline, dressed in the music that is proper to him, into Alvaro de Campos, all the emotion that I do not allow myself in my living. To think, my dear Casais Monteiro, that all these must be, in the act of publication, overtakers of Fernando Pessoa, impure and simple!

... I now go on to answer your question about the genesis of my heteronyms. You will see if I succeed in answering you completely. I begin with the psychiatric part. The origin of my heteronyms is at bottom an aspect of hysteria that exists in me. I don't know whether I am simply an hysteric or if I am more properly a neurasthenic hysteric. I tend toward the second hypothesis because there are in me evidences of lassitude that hysteria, properly speaking, doesn't encompass in the list of its symptoms. Be that as it may, the mental origin of my heteronyms lies in a persistent and organic tendency of mine toward depersonalization and simulation. These phenomena—happily for me and for others—intellectualize themselves in me; I mean, they don't show up in my practical life, either on the surface or in contact with others; they explode inside and I live with them alone inside me. If I were a woman (in women, hysterical phenomena erupt in attacks and similar ways), each poem of Alvaro de Campos (or, more hysterically hysterical, of mine) would cause a riot in the neighborhood. But I am a man—and for us men hysteria assumes mainly intellectual aspects; so it all ends up in silence and poetry.

This explains, *tant bien que mal*, the organic origin of my heteronyms. Now I'm going to tell you the straight story of my heteronyms. I begin with those who are dead, and with some I no longer remember—those that remain lost in the remote, almost forgotten past of my infancy. ... Sometime around 1912, unless I'm mistaken (which couldn't be very much), the idea came to me to write some poems of pagan character. I tried sketching some things in free verse (not in the style of Alvaro de Campos but in my own normal style), and then abandoned the attempt. But in that dim confusion I made out the hazy outline of the person that ... was writing. (Without my knowing it, Ricardo Reis had been born.) A year and a half or two years later, I remember one day taking up the challenge of Sá-Carneiro, to invent a bucolic poet,

of a complicated sort, and present him, I don't recall now how,
as if he were really a living creature. I spent a few days working
on him without getting anywhere. One day, just as I'd finally given
up—it was March 8, 1914—I went over to a high desk, and taking
a piece of paper, began to write, standing up, as I always do when
possible. And I wrote some thirty poems, one after another, in a
sort of ecstasy, the nature of which I'm unable to define. It was
the triumphant day of my life, and never will there be another
like it. I began with the title, *O Guadado Rebanhos (The Shepherd).*
What followed was the appearance of someone in me to whom I
immediately gave the name of Alberto Caeiro. Forgive me the
absurdity of the sentence: In me there appeared my master. That
was my immediate reaction. So much so that, scarcely were those
thirty-odd poems written when I took more paper and wrote,
again without stopping, the six poems constituting *Chuva Oblique
(Oblique Rain),* by Fernando Pessoa. Straight away and fully
formed . . . It was the return of Fernando Pessoa—Alberto
Caeiro to Fernando Pessoa himself. Or, better, it was the re-
action of Fernando Pessoa to his nonexistence as Alberto Caeiro.
Once Alberto Caeiro had appeared, I instinctively and subcon-
sciously tried to find disciples for him. Out of him I plucked the
false paganism latent in Richardo Reis; I discovered the name and
adapted it to him, because I had already seen him at that level.
And, suddenly, both stemming from and opposed to Ricardo Reis,
there impetuously arose in me a new individual. At once, and on
the typewriter, without interruption or correction, there surged up
the *Triumphal Ode* of Alvaro de Campos—the ode so entitled to-
gether with the man so named. Then I created a nonexistent
coterie. I fixed it all in real patterns. I gauged influences, I knew
the friendships, I heard inside me the discussions and divergences
of opinions, and in all this it seems to me that it was I, creator of
everything, that was least present. It seems that everything went
on independently of me. And it seems that it still goes on in this
way. If some day I can publish the esthetic conversations between
Ricardo Reis and Alvaro de Campos, you will see how different
they are and how I myself don't get into the matter.

When *Orpheu* was about to be published, it was necessary at
the last moment to delete something in order to come up with the
right number of pages. I then suggested to Sá-Carneiro that I put
in an "old" poem of Alvaro de Campos'—a poem of what Alvaro

de Campos would have been like before he'd known Caiero and had fallen under his influence. And so I made *Opiario,* in which I attempted to present all the latent tendencies of Alvaro de Campos, in keeping with what would be revealed later, but without having yet any hint of contact with his master Caeiro. It was out of the poems that I have written, or that I gave myself to make, in the double power of depersonalization that I had to develop. But, finally, I believe that it didn't come out badly and that it shows Alvaro in the bud . . .

. . . I think I've explained to you the origin of my heteronyms. However, there remains some point about which it is necessary to give a more lucid understanding—I am writing fast, and when I write fast I am not very lucid—I mean, that in good time I will give this to you. And it's true, a real complement of this is the hysterical; in writing certain passages of the Notes remembering my master Caeiro through Alvaro de Campos, I have wept real tears. It is for you to know with whom you are coping, my dear Casais Monteiro!

But some points about this matter. I saw within me, in a color-less space more real than a dream, the faces, gestures, of Caeiro, Ricardo Reis and Alvaro de Campos. I made out their ages and their lives. Ricardo Reis was born in 1887, not that I remember the day and the month (though I have them somewhere), in Porto, is a doctor and is living at present in Brazil. Alberto Caeiro was born in 1889 and died in 1915; he was born in Lisbon, but lived almost all his life in the country. He had neither profession nor any sort of education. Alvaro de Campos was born in Tavira, on the fifteenth of October 1890 (at 1:30 P.M., Gerreira Gomes tells me; and it is true, since it is certain that a horoscope was made of this hour.) As you know, he is a naval engineer (in Glasgow), but now living here in Lisbon, retired. Caeiro is of medium height, and, though really delicate (he died a consumptive), he didn't seem as delicate as he was. Ricardo Reis is a bit, though very slightly, shorter, stronger, sallower. Alvaro de Campos is tall (1.75 meters tall, two centimeters taller than I), drawn, and with a tendency to a slight stoop. All are clean-shaven—Caeiro pale without color, blue eyes; Reis a vague dull brown; Campos between fair and swarthy, a vaguely Jewish Portuguese type, hair therefore smooth and normally parted on the side, monocled. Caeiro, as I said, hasn't any education to speak of—only primary grade; his father and mother died and left him a house, where he lived on the income of a few small properties. He lived with an old aunt, on his mother's side. Ricardo Reis, educated in a Jesuit college, is, as I said, a doctor; he's been living in Brazil since 1919; for he became an expatriate immediately because he was a monarchist. He is a Latinist by virtue of school training, and a semi-Hellenist by virtue of his own training. Alvaro de Campos has a highschool education; he later went to Scotland to study engineering, first mechanical, then naval. On some holiday he went to the Orient, from which *Opiário* resulted. An uncle taught him Latin, when he was verging on becoming a priest.

How do I write under three names? . . . Caeiro, by way of pure and unexpected inspiration, without knowing or deliberately thinking of what I would write. Ricardo Reis, after some abstract deliberation, that suddenly concretizes itself in an ode. Campos, when I feel a sudden impulse to write and don't know what. (My semi-heteronym Bernardo Soares, who in many ways resembles Alvaro de Campos, seems always to be tired or sleepy, so that his powers of ratiocination and inhibition are slightly suspended; he writes prose in a constant daydream. He is a semi-heteronym because, not being a personality to me, he is not so much different from myself as a simple distortion of my personality. It is I, less rational and emotional. His prose, because his reasoning somewhat resembles mine, is like mine, and is a perfectly adequate Portuguese; Caeiro wrote Portuguese badly, Campos reasonably but with lapses, as when he would say *eu proprio* instead of *eu mesmo,* etc., Reis better than I, but with a puristic streak I regard as exaggerated. It is difficult for me to write the prose of Reis . . . or of de Campos. To simulate in verse is easier, since it is more spontaneous."

Páginas de Doutrina Estética, 259-260

From "Notes in Memory of My Master Caeiro Signed by Alvaro de Campos"

"My master Caeiro was not a pagan; he was paganism. Ricardo Reis is a pagan, António Mora is a pagan, I am a pagan. Fernando Pessoa himself would be a pagan if he weren't so balled up inside himself. But Ricardo Reis is a pagan by virtue of character, António Mora a pagan by virtue of intelligence, I am a pagan by virtue of my rebelliousness, that is, by temperament. In Caeiro there was no explanation for paganism; he had been consubstantiated."

*Notas para a recordação de meu mestre Caeiro
assinadas por Alvaro de Campos*

(From Fernando Pessoa's Letters to Armando Cortes Rodrigues)

"I maintain it's clear—my object of launching pseudonymously the work of Caeiro-Reis-Campos. This is all a literature that I created and lived (that's sincere because it is felt) whereby I created a current of possible influence, incontestably beneficial in the hearts of others. What I call insincere literature is not analogous to that of Alberto Caeiro, Ricard Reis, or Alvaro de Campos ... it is written dramatically but is sincere (in my grave sense of the word) as what King Lear says is sincere, that is not Shakespeare but ... a creation of his. I call things insincere that are made to astonish, and things, likewise—note this, it's important—that don't have in them a fundamental metaphysical idea: that is, through which there doesn't pass, like a wind, a notion of the gravity and mystery of life. That's why everything I write under the names of Caeiro, Reis, Alvaro de Campos is serious. In any of them I put a profound conceptual life, different in all three, but in all gravely attentive to the mysterious importance of existence."

from *Cartas de Fernando Pessoa a Armando Cortes
Rodrigues,* pp. 2-3.

Some Biographical Dates

1888. Born Fernando António Nogueira Pessoa, June 13, in
Lisbon.

1893. Father, Joaquim de Seabra Pessoa, dies July 13, at 43.

1895. Mother, Maria Madalena Pinheiro Nogueira Pessoa, marries
by proxy João Miguel Rosa, appointed Portuguese Consul
to South Africa, and joins him with her children, in-
cluding Fernando, the following year in Durban.

1899. Fernando enrolled as a student in Durban High School.

1905. He returns to Lisbon alone, and registers the following
year at the University in Lisbon.

1907. He withdraws from the university and sets up a print-
shop business, which fails.

1908. He begins long part-time career as commercial letter-
writer and translator.

1912. Publishes first article, "The New Portuguese Poetry,
Sociologically Considered," in *A Águia,* principal organ
of the Portuguese Renaissance group. A second article,
"The New Portuguese Poetry in its Psychological Aspect,"
appears later the same year.

1913. Writes the English poem, "Epithalamium," and in Por-
tuguese, the closet drama, *O Marinheiro (The Sailor).*

1914. The advent of three heteronyms, Alberto Caeiro, Alvaro
de Campos, and Ricardo Reis, with their first poems.

1915. Writes the English poem, "Antinous," and in Portuguese,
"Salutation to Walt Whitman."

1916. His close friend, the poet Mário Sá-Carneiro, commits
suicide in Paris.

1918. He publishes privately in Lisbon two pamphlets of
English poems, *Antinous* and *35 Sonnets.*

1920. His English poem, "Meantime," appears in *The Athenaeum*
(London), and he finishes a group of English poems,
"Inscriptions."

1925. His mother dies.

1926. He applies for a patent on his invention: *Synthetic
Yearly Calendar By Name and Any Other Classification,
Consultable in Any Language.*

1927. José Régio (Portugal's best-known surviving poet) publishes in *Presença* the first critical article on the new poetry to single out the work of "the master," Fernando Pessoa.

1928. A full-length study of the poet's personality appears in *Temas,* a book by João Gaspar Simões, who becomes Pessoa's biographer (in two volumes, *Vida e Obra de Fernando Pessoa,* Lisbon, n.d.).

1930. Starts a correspondence with Aleister Crowley in London.

1933. Undergoes severe psychological crisis.

1934. Wins second prize for poem-sequence, *Mensagem,* published the same year.

1935. Dies on November 30 of hepatitis in the Hospital de S. Luís, Lisbon.